The SEND CODE of PRACTICE 0-25 YEARS

SAGE was founded in 1965 by Sara Miller McCune to
support the dissemination of usable knowledge by publishing
innovative and high-quality research and teaching content.
Today, we publish more than 750 journals, including those
of more than 300 learned societies, more than 800 new
books per year, and a growing range of library products
including archives, data, case studies, reports, conference
highlights, and video. SAGE remains majority-owned by our
founder, and after Sara's lifetime will become owned by a
charitable trust that secures our continued independence.

Los Angeles | London | New Delhi | Singapore | Washington DC | Boston

The

SEND
CODE
of PRACTICE

0–25
YEARS

Policy, Provision & Practice

RONA TUTT & PAUL WILLIAMS

Los Angeles | London | New Delhi
Singapore | Washington DC | Boston

Los Angeles | London | New Delhi
Singapore | Washington DC | Boston

SAGE Publications Ltd
1 Oliver's Yard
55 City Road
London EC1Y 1SP

SAGE Publications Inc.
2455 Teller Road
Thousand Oaks, California 91320

SAGE Publications India Pvt Ltd
B 1/I 1 Mohan Cooperative Industrial Area
Mathura Road
New Delhi 110 044

SAGE Publications Asia-Pacific Pte Ltd
3 Church Street
#10-04 Samsung Hub
Singapore 049483

Commissioning editor: Amy Jarrold
Editorial assistant: George Knowles
Project manager: Jeanette Graham
Production editor: Nicola Marshall
Copyeditor: Rosemary Campbell
Proofreader: Isabel Kirkwood
Indexer: Rona Tutt and Paul Williams
Marketing executive: Dilhara Attygalle
Cover design: Wendy Scott
Typeset by: C&M Digitals (P) Ltd, Chennai, India
Printed in India by Replika Press Pvt Ltd

Library of Congress Control Number: 2014957494

British Library Cataloguing in Publication data

A catalogue record for this book is available from the British Library

ISBN 978-1-47390-796-6
ISBN 978-1-47390-797-3 (pbk)

FSC
MIX
Paper from responsible sources
FSC® C016779
www.fsc.org

At SAGE we take sustainability seriously. Most of our products are printed in the UK using FSC papers and boards. When we print overseas we ensure sustainable papers are used as measured by the Egmont grading system. We undertake an annual audit to monitor our sustainability.

We would like to dedicate this book to all those who are trying to ensure that the SEND Code of Practice 2015 leads to better outcomes for children, young people and their families.

Contents

About the Authors

Dr Rona Tutt OBE has taught pupils of all ages in state and independent, day and residential, mainstream and special schools. She has been a winner of the Leadership in Teaching Award, received an Outstanding Reviewer Award for her work on the *International Journal of Educational Management* and an OBE for her services to special needs education. She is a Past President of the National Association of Head Teachers (NAHT) and continues to be involved in their work, particularly in the field of SEND.

Since the Green Paper, *Support and Aspiration: A New Approach to Special Educational Needs and Disabilities* (DfE, 2011) was launched, Rona has been in constant demand as a speaker on the changes to the SEN Framework. She is vice chair of governors at two schools in a local authority which is an SEND Pathfinder. She has been on the Expert Reference Group of the Autism Education Trust (AET), which is mentioned in Annex B of the *SEND Code of Practice 2015*, since its inception.

Rona is the author of *Every Child Included* (2007); she co-authored *Educating Children with Complex Conditions: Understanding Overlapping and Co-existing Developmental Disorders* (Dittrich and Tutt, 2008); and wrote *Partnership Working to Support Special Educational Needs and Disabilities* in 2010.

Paul Williams was born in Newcastle upon Tyne, but has been a resident of London since becoming a teacher in 1973 and working in Inner London comprehensive schools until 1987. He was an advisory teacher with ILEA until 1989, after which he was a deputy head until 1992. He has been a head teacher since 1992 of two London special schools – most recently in Harrow. Paul is a national leader of education (NLE) and his school is a national support school (NSS). He is chair of Harrow's Alternative Provision Governing Body and vice-chair of Harrow Mencap.

Paul has been a member of NAHT's National Executive since 2006 and has chaired the Association's SEND Committee since 2008. He has been involved with a wide range of national reviews, consultations and developments. He gave evidence to Lord Bew's Independent Review of Key Stage 2

Testing, Assessment and Accountability (2011) was involved in the review of the national curriculum, and has contributed to the All Party Parliamentary Group on Autism (APPGA).

Paul attends regular meetings with Ofsted and the DfE, most recently in connection with how pupils with SEND are to be assessed under the new national curriculum, and the *Independent review of standards for teaching assistants*.

This is the second book that Paul and Rona have co-authored, the first being *How Successful Schools Work: The Impact of Innovative School Leadership*, which was published in 2012.

Acknowledgements

We would like to offer our sincere thanks to all the people, schools, settings and services who gave up their time to talk to us, allowed us to visit, or to highlight their work in this book. They are:

Tim Bowen	Head teacher, Maple Primary School, Hertfordshire
Richard Boyle	Head teacher, Muntham House School, West Sussex
Jamie Bargeman	Whitefield Schools and Centre
David Bartram	Director of Inclusion, Lampton School, Hounslow
Jane Carter	Head of Teaching & Learning, Integrated Disability Service, Warwickshire CC
Kay Charles	Head teacher, The Village School, Brent
Janine Cherrington	Head of Service Transition 2, St Andrews School, Derby
Elaine Colquhoun	Executive Principal, Whitefield Schools and Centre, Walthamstow
Harry Dicks	Somerset Association of Heads of Specialist Provision
Tony Draper	Head teacher, Water Hall Primary School, Milton Keynes
Jonathan Fawcett	Head teacher, Swanwick Hall, Derbyshire
John Galligan	School Improvement Team Manager, Brent Council
Sharon Gray	Head teacher, Netherfield Primary School, Nottingham
Phil Harrison	Head teacher, St Andrews School, Derby
Helen Hewitt	Chief Executive, Chailey Heritage Foundation
Anne Hill	Early Years SEND Manager, Herts CC
Cassie Howe	Advisory Team, New Schools Network

Janice Howkins	Head teacher, Bentley Wood High School, Harrow
Kim Johnson	Head teacher, Bradfields Academy, Medway
Amanda King	Head teacher, Bedworth Heath Nursery School and Children's Centre, Warwickshire
Desi Lodge Patch	Head teacher, Woodfield School, Brent
Jan Martin	Director of SENsitive Education Consultancy
Nicole McCartney	Executive Principal, Ormiston Venture Academy, Great Yarmouth
Karen Milton	Head teacher, Selworthy School, Taunton
Seamus Oates	Executive head teacher, Tri-borough Alternative Provision, London
Debbie Orton	Head of Integrated Services for Learning, Herts CC
Jac Raggozino	Acting SENCO, Water Hall Primary School, Milton Keynes
Dr John Reavley	Executive head teacher, The Jubilee Academy, Harrow
Malcolm Reeve	National Director of Education for Special Needs & Disabilities, Academies Enterprise Trust
Angela Smith	Team Leader, FAST Team, Selworthy School, Taunton
Sarah Vize	Transport Strategy & Policy Manager, Herts CC

Abbreviations and Acronyms

AAA	Ambitious about Autism
ADHD	Attention deficit hyperactivity disorder
AET	Autism Education Trust
AP	Alternative Provision
ASD	Autistic spectrum disorder
BESD	Behaviour, emotional and social development
BSF	Building Schools for the Future
CALM	Crisis, aggression, limitation and management
CAMHS	Children and Adolescent Mental Health Service
CCGs	Clinical Commissioning Groups
CDC	Council for Disabled Children
CEO	Chief Education Officer
CLDD	Complex learning difficulties and disabilities
CP	Challenge Partnership
CPD	Continuing professional development
CTC	City technology college
DCO	Designated Clinical Officer
DDA	Disability Discrimination Act
DMO	Designated Medical Officer
DSPL	Developing Special Provision Locally
EAL	English as an additional language
ECM	Every Child Matters

EHC Plan	Education, Health and Care Plan
EP	Educational psychologist
ESA	Employment and Support Allowance
EYFS	Early years foundation stage
FASD	Foetal alcohol spectrum disorder
FE	Further Education
FSM	Free school meals
HE	Higher education
HI	Hearing impairment
HLTAs	High level teaching assistants
IASS	Information, Advice and Support Service
IDP	Inclusion development programme
IEP	Individual Education Plan
IHCP	Individual Healthcare Plan
ITT	Initial teacher training
JSNA	Joint Strategic Needs Assessment
LAC	Looked after children
LDA	Learning Difficulty Assessment
LDD	Learning difficulties and disabilities
LEA	Local education authority
LLE	Local leader of education
LPPA	Leading Parent Partnership Award
LSCB	Local Safeguarding Children's Board
MAT	Multi-Academy Trust
MLD	Moderate learning difficulties
MSI	Multi-sensory impairments
NAHT	National Association of Head Teachers
NAS	National Autistic Society
NASAT	National Autistic Society Academies Trust
NASEN	National Association for Special Educational Needs
NCC	Norfolk County Council

NCTL	National College of Teaching and Leadership
NEET	Not in Education, Employment or Training
NCB	National Children's Bureau
NHS	National Health Service
NLE	National leader of education
NLG	National leader of governance
NNPCF	National Network of Parent Carer Forums
NSN	New Schools Network
NSS	National support school
OAT	Ormiston Academies Trust
Ofsted	Office for standards in education
PAN	Published admission number
PCF	Parent carer forum
PCT	Primary Care Trust
PDA	Pathological demand avoidance syndrome
PGCE	Postgraduate certificate of education
PLTS	Personal, learning and thinking skills
PMLD	Profound and multiple learning difficulties
PPS	Parent Partnership Services
PRU	Pupil referral unit
PRUsAP	Pupil Referral Units & Alternative Provision
PSCHE	Personal, social, citizenship and health education
QTLS	Qualified teacher learning and skills
QTS	Qualified teacher status
RARPA	Recognising and Rewarding Progress and Achievement
RPA	Raising the Participation Age
SaLT	Speech and language therapist
SCITT	School-centred initial teacher training
SDQ	Strengths and Difficulties Questionnaire
SEMH	Social, emotional and mental health difficulties
SEN	Special educational needs
SENCO	Special educational needs co-ordinator

SEND	Special educational needs and disability
SENDA	Special Educational Needs Disability Act
SFR	Statistical first release
SLCN	Speech, language and communication needs
SpLD	Specific learning difficulties
SLD	Severe learning difficulties
SLE	Specialist leader of education
SLI	Specific language impairment
SLT	Senior leadership team
STEM	Science, technology, engineering and maths
SWELTEC	South West London Teachers Education Consortium
TA	Teaching assistant
TBAP	Tri-borough Alternative Provision
TaMHS	Targeted Mental Health in Schools
UTC	University Technical Colleges
VCS	Voluntary and community sector
VI	Visual impairment

How to Use this Book

This book has been written to explain the changes to the SEN Framework resulting from the Children and Families Act 2014 and set out in the *Special Educational Needs and Disability Code of Practice: 0 to 25 years* (DfE/DoH, 2015). The Code contains statutory guidance for all those who work with and support children and young people who have special educational needs and disabilities throughout the 0–25 age range.

As it is important to understand both what has changed and how this is designed to create a change in culture, the book is divided into three parts. Following an introductory chapter, the first part explains how the SEN system has changed and the other two parts focus on how professionals in early years, schools and post-16 settings, are working with local authorities, pupils, parents and professionals in other services to implement the changes in line with the SEND Code.

Part One: Policy concentrates on how the policy around children and young people with special needs and their families changed from the autumn of 2014 onwards.

- Chapter 1 outlines the background to the changes and why they were felt to be necessary.
- Chapter 2 looks at the work of the SEND Pathfinder authorities that piloted the changes.
- Chapter 3 provides an overview of the chapters of the SEND Code and its two annexes.

Part Two: Provision moves on to look at how provision, in terms of the physical environment, the closer working between education, health and social care services, and the increase in the age range up to 25 years, is reflected in case studies across the services and across the extended age range.

- Chapter 4 looks at the growth of specialist provision in a variety of educational settings.
- Chapter 5 explains how local authorities (LAs) and schools are working together in the wake of the SEND pathfinders' experience.

- Chapter 6 concentrates on the development of specialist provision up to 25 years.

Part Three: Practice describes how the SEND Code of Practice is being interpreted across mainstream, specialist and alternative provision, in terms of the support offered to children, young people and their families.

- Chapter 7 describes some of the different ways mainstream settings are meeting the needs of a wider range of pupils.
- Chapter 8 looks at how special and alternative provision is adapting to meet the needs of young learners at the most complex end of the SEN continuum.
- Chapter 9 considers how the workforce is being trained to meet the demands resulting from the SEND Code of Practice.

The concluding chapter draws out some of the lessons from the previous chapters, in terms of how to effect the change in culture that lies at the heart of the reforms, including how to ensure that all teachers see themselves as teachers of all pupils, and how to place children, young people and their families at the heart of the decision-making process.

The chapters include the following features:

- An overview of the chapter
- Key points of information
- Questions for reflection
- Activities
- Case studies
- Suggestions for further reading, which includes references to relevant parts of the SEND Code of Practice.

Although it is possible to dip in and out of the book according to what catches the reader's interest, for those who are not familiar with the changes since the *2001 SEN Code of Practice* the rest of the book will make more sense if the information in Part 1 is read first.

NB As the book is based on the *Special Educational Needs and Disability Code of Practice: 0 to 25 years* (DfE/DoH, 2015), it is referred to many times. To save giving the title in full each time, it is sometimes abbreviated to the 'SEND Code of Practice 2015', or simply the 'SEND Code'. Where reference is made to the SEND Code of Practice that was briefly in place between September 2014 and March 2015, it will be referred to as the SEND Code of Practice 2014. You can access the full *SEND Code of Practice: 0-25 Years* online via https://www.gov.uk/government/publications/send-code-of-practice-0-to-25

Note to the Reader

This book is based on the SEND Code of Practice that was published in January 2015.

To avoid any confusion, below is an explanation about the SEN / SEND Codes of Practice that were in use between 2001 and 2015 when this book was written.

The Special Educational Needs Code of Practice that was published in November 2001 by the Department for Education and Skills (DfES) remained in use until August 2014. However, the section of this Code describing the statementing procedures may remain relevant until March 2018, by which time all statements are due to have been replaced by Education, Health and Care Plans (EHC Plans).

In July 2014, the *Special educational needs and disability code of practice: 0–25 Years* was published jointly by the Department of Education (DfE) and the Department of Health (DoH). It came into force on 1st September 2014. However, it was only in place until the end of March 2015.

In January 2015, another version of the July 2014 Code was published and came into effect from 1st April 2015. Apart from Chapter 10, which is entitled *Children and Young Persons in Specific Circumstances*, and has additional information about children and young people who have SEN and are in youth custody, there are very few differences between the July 2014 Code and the January 2015 Code.

Introduction

Chapter overview

This chapter seeks to set the scene for the rest of the book by:

- Explaining the climate at the time the SEND Code of Practice 2014 was implemented
- Introducing the headline changes in the new SEN system
- Outlining the main changes for schools and other educational settings
- Touching on the increase in the pupil population and on the complexity of some pupils' needs.

It explains how these themes are developed in the rest of the book, and how, when taken together, the changes represent a change in culture which may take many years to come to fruition.

The climate for change

Between autumn 2010, when the changes to the SEN Framework began to be developed, and September 2014, when they started to be implemented, many other events occurred. First of all, the economic climate altered and budgets for everyone became much tighter. Secondly, the impact on schools of changes to the national curriculum and its assessment, together with the changes to the examination system, meant that schools were dealing with a number of fundamental changes as well as a new SEND Code of Practice (*Special Educational Needs and Disability Code of practice: 0 to 25 years*, published July 2014 and updated in January 2015 – see note on opposite page).

Another aspect of change that affected the implementation of the new SEN Framework, was the acceleration of what has been called the 'academisation' of schools. The move to encourage schools to become academies altered the relationship between local authorities (LAs) and their schools, as academies are independent of the LAs in which they are situated. Academisation, combined with financial constraints, made it harder for LAs to maintain its staff and services, while being expected, under the changes to the SEN system, to take on new responsibilities.

So, while the timing of the changes around SEN and disability (SEND) could be seen as less than ideal, there was a more positive side. The lead up to the Children and Families Act (2014) and the final version of the SEND Code of Practice meant that, for three or four years, SEND had a higher than usual profile. During this time, parental expectations were raised, without, perhaps, the realisation that the changes would take time to be implemented and to have an effect.

The main changes to the SEN system

The changes to the SEN Framework are sometimes referred to as the biggest shake up of the system since the Warnock Report of 1978. (There is a fuller account of the background to the changes in the next chapter.) What it is important to say at the outset is that the changes place children, young people and their families at the heart of the process. This is both in terms of being involved in the decisions that affect them and the wider expectation that, through having their voices heard, they will be in a position to influence the SEN system as a whole and to help it improve. In chapter 1 of the SEND Code of Practice 2015, the first principle states that LAs must have regard to 'the views, wishes and feelings of the child or young person, and the child's parents' (paragraph 1.1).

Another main theme is the need for education, health and social care to work more closely together. Many children and young people, whatever the nature of their barriers to learning, may need the input of more than one service. All will need support to make the most of their education, but many will also need support from the health service or from social care, and some will need the involvement of all three services. The SEND Code describes how LAs and local clinical commissioning groups (CCGs) will need to have a co-ordinated approach to working with each other and with families. One demonstration of this, is replacing statements with Education, Health and Care Plans (EHC Plans). As the SEN system now extends to young people up to 25 years of age, EHC Plans will be for those who are over 16 as well and will replace learning difficulty assessments (LDAs).

Unlike the change from statements to EHC Plans, which continues the idea of giving protection to learners with the most significant needs, asking LAs to develop a Local Offer is something entirely new. It arose out of the many meetings Sarah Teather had with parents and carers when she was the Minister responsible for special needs. When the Green Paper, *Support and Aspiration: A New Approach to SEND* (DfE, 2011a) was being discussed, in the lead up to the Children and Families Act (DfE, 2014a), they told her many times how difficult it was to find the information they needed. Sarah Teather's idea was that the Local Offer would overcome this difficulty, by putting all the information families needed in one place. To assemble the information was a considerable task for LAs, but by September 2014, the Local Offer was up and running on LAs' websites. The intention is that it will continue to grow and develop, with the active involvement of all concerned.

With the age range covered by the SEND Code increasing to 25 years of age, there is a focus on preparation for adulthood from the start. This ties in with an emphasis on having high aspirations for every learner, however complex their needs, and considering the outcomes young people and their families want to achieve. The Code stresses that, as soon as a child is identified as having SEN, families need to be reassured that the majority of young people will be able to work, to live independently and to take part in their local communities.

Changes for education

As far as those working in schools and other educational settings are concerned, the central change is around all teachers seeing themselves as teachers who have responsibility for the progress and well-being of every child in their class, including those who have SEND. While special educational needs co-ordinators (SENCOs) are seen as having a vital role in supporting colleagues, their role is a more strategic one, concerned with developing the school's SEN Policy, overseeing its implementation and discussing provision and resources with the head teacher and governing body.

The change from having the two-tier system of school action and school action plus, to the single category of SEN support is not meant to be a way of reducing the number of pupils being identified as having SEN. However, it is seen as an opportunity to make sure that high quality teaching is in place, before it is assumed that a child has special needs. The change in terminology also means that specialists can be brought in at any stage rather than having to wait for a pupil to be moved from school action to school action plus.

Three of the four broad headings of need remain in place from the 2001 SEN Code of Practice. These are:

- Communication and interaction
- Cognition and learning
- Sensory and/or physical needs.

The one that has changed is 'behaviour, emotional and social development' (BESD) which has been replaced by 'social, emotional and mental health difficulties' (SEMH). This is partly to encourage people to look behind the behaviour to what is causing it and partly to recognise the importance of mental health issues, in case they are a factor in the difficulties the pupil is experiencing.

A growing and complex pupil population

As part of the context in which these changes are taking place, this book looks at the growth in the pupil population as a whole, particularly at the younger end, and also at the growing complexity of pupils' needs. Although the SEND Code does not tackle this head on, as well as raising the need to consider children's mental health, it also places a greater emphasis than in the 2001 SEN Code on medical conditions, in recognition of the fact that many mainstream schools are now educating children with quite complex medical needs.

Interpreting the SEND Code of Practice

This chapter has mentioned very briefly some of the important changes being brought about by the 2014 SEND Code of Practice, which started to be implemented from September 2014, and the January 2015 version which replaced it from April 2015. In Part 1 of this book, there is a much fuller explanation about the background to the changes and what they mean. Parts 2 and 3 are built around case studies of schools and other settings, showing how they are adapting or developing their provision and practice in line with the demands of the 2014 SEND Code. These examples help to illustrate how different settings affect practice and therefore have an impact on outcomes for children and young people. What they do not show is that there is a right way of putting policy into practice, but that every setting and every learner within each setting is different and that their needs can be addressed in a variety of ways.

The Department for Education (DfE) and the Department of Health (DoH) have laid down timescales for implementing the changes between September 2014 and April 2018 (see *Implementing a New 0 to 25 Special Needs System: LAs and Partners. Duties and Timescales – What you Must Do and When* (DfE/DoH, 2014c). What may take even longer to put in place is the change in culture that the changes are designed to bring about.

PART ONE

POLICY

How the SEN Framework changed

Chapter overview

This chapter traces the background to the changes that started to be implemented from September 2014, in line with the 2014 and 2015 SENDs Codes of Practice. It outlines how SEN has evolved since the time of Warnock and the 1981 Education Act.

It explains how the Codes themselves have changed from the five-stage model of the first code, to the four-stage model of the code that was in existence from 2001 to August 2014.

It states why a change to the SEN Framework which necessitated a new SEND Code of Practice was thought to be necessary and what the changes hoped to achieve.

The background

The year 2014 was a landmark in the lives of young people who have special educational needs or disabilities (SEND) and their families, as it heralded the most comprehensive overhaul of the system for over 30 years. The change in the way the special needs system operates was a result of the Children and Families Act (2014), which meant that a new SEND Code of Practice needed to be written and implemented from September 2014. To understand the significance of a change that has been described as the biggest shake-up of the system for over 30 years, it may be helpful to start with a reminder of the SEN Framework that had been in place since the 1980s.

How the previous system arose

A few years after the Education Act of 1970, which brought all children into the education system for the first time, Mary Warnock (who later became Baroness Warnock), was invited by the government of the day to chair a committee to look into the education that 'handicapped' children (as they were described at the time) were receiving. Subsequently, the *Report of the Committee of Enquiry into the Education of Handicapped Children and Young People* (DES, 1978) was published. It was the work of this committee that resulted in the term 'handicapped' being replaced by 'special educational needs'.

The Warnock Committee's use of the term 'SEN' was partly to move away from concentrating too heavily on placing a child with a handicap in a category of need, ('educationally subnormal' and 'maladjusted' were two of the terms used at the time), rather than seeing each child as an individual who has individual needs. Secondly, the term SEN was used to encompass a much wider range of pupils who, although their needs may be less significant, still benefit from support to overcome any barriers to learning.

The Report resulted in the Education Act of 1981, which is remembered largely for setting out the statementing procedures that remained in place until statements were replaced by Education, Health and Care Plans (EHC Plans) from September 2014. This was a well-intentioned move to safeguard the provision for the 2% or so of pupils with the most complex needs. The downside was that it did little to take on board the needs of the 18% identified by Warnock as having less complex special needs, but still requiring some support.

The first SEN Code of Practice

However, the needs of the whole SEN continuum were addressed in the first version of the SEN Code of Practice which was published in 1994 (*Code of Practice on the Identification and Assessment of Special Educational Needs* (DfE, 1994)). This set out a five-stage model:

Stage 1   Following initial concerns by a teacher, parent, or professional from health or social services, the child should be placed on an SEN register and receive support within the classroom.

Stage 2   If insufficient progress is being made, the special educational needs co-ordinator (SENCO) should be involved and an Individual Education Plan (IEP) drawn up.

Stage 3   Where there is still a lack of progress, the Local Education Authority (LEA) should be informed and Support Services consulted, who help to draw up a new IEP.

Stage 4   If the concerns continue, the pupil should be considered for a formal assessment, which the LEA carries out if it is felt that the child might need a statement.

Stage 5 If, following the formal assessment, the LEA decides that it needs to determine the special educational provision the child needs, a statement of special educational needs will be drawn up.

The Code also outlined the role of the SENCO and assumed that this would be 'a designated teacher' (paragraph 2.14). When the Code was updated in 2001, it was suggested that the role should be viewed as equivalent to a literacy or numeracy co-ordinator in a primary school, or a head of department or head of year in a secondary school.

A change of century and a second code of practice

The turn of the century saw two significant events: the 2001 Special Educational Needs and Disability Act (sometimes referred to as 'SENDA') and, in the same year, *Special Educational Needs: Code of Practice* (DfES, 2001b), which was an updated version of the 1994 Code. After the Act, 'SEN' was replaced increasingly by 'SEN and disability' or SEND. However the overlap between SEN and disability has never been clearly defined, so both SEN and SEND continue to be used.

The 2001 Code of Practice described children's needs under four broad headings:

1. Communication and interaction
2. Cognition and learning
3. Behaviour, emotional and social development (BESD)
4. Physical or sensory impairment.

As mentioned previously, three of these have been retained in the current Code, with BESD being replaced by 'Social, emotional and mental health difficulties'. The reasons behind this change are given in Chapter 3 of this book and comments on the change from BESD to SEMH appear as part of the case studies in Parts 2 and 3.

The Code also reduced the graduated response from five to four stages, although the terminology of stages was no longer used. Putting pupils on an SEN register was no longer seen as a necessary first step, although many schools continued to have a register. Stages two and three became School Action and School Action Plus:

School Action A child is put on this level if s/he is making inadequate progress and needs interventions that are additional to, or different from, those provided as part of a differentiated curriculum. These could be recorded in a Group Education Plan rather than an IEP, if a group of children needed similar support.

School Action Plus The child is moved on to this next stage if progress is still insufficient and the school feels the need to call on outside agencies for further advice and support.

The final two stages of Statutory Assessment and Statementing remained as before.

Developments between 2002 and 2010

Although there was no major review of the SEN Framework between the Warnock Report and the build-up to the Children and Families Act 2014, there were many developments affecting children and young people with special needs and those who support them.

In 2003, Cathy Ashton (now Baroness Ashton), who was the Minister for SEN at the time, established a special schools working group (see The Report of the Special Schools Working Group 2003) to consider their future role. This fed into the Labour government's *Removing Barriers to Achievement: The Government's Strategy for SEN* (DfES, 2004). It suggested that special schools might educate fewer children, as teachers in mainstream schools became more used to educating pupils with a wider range of needs. Yet, when Andrew Adonis (Lord Adonis), who, by then, was Minister for SEN, was asked by the Education and Skills Committee a couple of years later (see Special Educational Needs, Vol 3 2005/ 06) whether this was still the case, he replied that the government wanted to support having 'a flexible range of provision' and would be content for special school places to remain at their current level. Subsequently, the Department produced *Planning and Developing Special Educational Provision: A Guide for Local Authorities and Other Proposers* (DCSF, 2007) setting out what a continuum of provision should cover.

Although there were no major changes to the overall framework, the significance of the role of SENCOs was increasingly recognised, first by legislation in 2008 requiring them to be qualified teachers and secondly, by introducing a mandatory qualification for them.

Key point: SENCOs' qualifications

2008   Legislation was introduced stating that anyone taking on the role of SENCO must be a qualified teacher.

2009   From this date, it became law for every new SENCO to gain the Masters-level National Award for SEN Co-ordination within 3 years of taking up the post.

2014   In line with the *SEND Code of Practice: 0 to 25 Years*, from 1 September, revised learning outcomes for the Award replaced the previous ones. (See National College for Teaching and Leadership (2014) *National Award for SEN Co-ordination: Learning Outcomes*.)

Towards the end of the Labour government's 10 years in office, the profile of SEN gathered momentum and a series of reports were issued into different types and aspects of SEN. Significant among these, in terms of their influence on the coming changes, were the *Lamb Inquiry: Special Educational Needs and Parental Confidence* (DCSF, 2009) and Ofsted's *The Special Educational Needs and Disability Review: A Statement is not Enough* (Ofsted, 2010).

In the foreword to Brian Lamb's Inquiry, he said that, in gathering the views of parents, he had 'met some of the happiest parents in the country and some of the angriest'. He summed up the four areas where change was most needed as:

1. Putting outcomes for children at the heart of the system
2. Giving parents a stronger voice
3. Focusing on children's needs and not waiting for them to fail before providing the help they need
4. Strengthening the voice of children.

All these comments are reflected in the changes to the SEN Framework.

The Ofsted Review 2010 criticised schools for the over-identification of SEND. Whether or not it is a coincidence or partly as a result of Ofsted's comments, the number of pupils with special needs has dropped since then (see Chapter 5 of this book for a fuller explanation). The review also said that: '... no one model – such as special schools, full inclusion in mainstream settings, or specialist units co-located with mainstream settings – worked better than any other' (Executive summary, Ofsted, 2010: 7). This is borne out by the case studies in this book, which show effective practice across a range of very different settings.

Questions for reflection

1. What do you think about Ofsted's comment that teachers over-identify pupils with SEN?
2. What are your reasons for agreeing or disagreeing with what the Ofsted Inspectors wrote?
3. How difficult do you think it is to identify which pupils have special needs, when SEN is a continuum, which, at the milder end, merges into the rest of the school population?

Why change was necessary

According to the government in the Information Pack produced for school leaders in July 2014 (*A DfE Presentation Pack for School Leaders: The 0–25 Special Educational Needs and Disability Reforms* (DfE, 2014b)), change was necessary because the previous system was too complicated. It was expensive and yet it delivered poor outcomes; in other words, it did not represent value for money. Under this general statement, the following points were made:

Parents struggle to find the services to help them and they have to tell their stories over and over again.

The difficulty of where to find the help parents need has led to the Local Offer, where all the information can be found in one place. Education, Health and Care Plans (EHC Plans) are designed to enable parents to tell their story once and not have to retell it to different people, as professionals across all the services should be working more closely together.

Moving from children's to adults' services can be very difficult.

Extending the age range to 25 years and having one system for pre-16 and post-16 should make this a seamless transition.

Despite spending over £5 billion a year on SEND provision, those with special needs are less likely to do well at GCSE and more likely to be NEETs (Not in Education, Employment or Training).

While it may well be true that not all the money that is expended on children and young people with special needs is spent as effectively as it might be, the comment about pupils with SEND doing less well at GCSE seems a strange one. Certainly, the hope must be that the changes to the SEN Framework result in more learners reaching their potential. While it is possible to have SEND and to be sufficiently academic to move on to Higher Education, or, indeed, to have exceptional gifts, the fact remains that students with special needs will have general or specific learning difficulties, or other barriers to learning. While the right provision and education can, and does, make an enormous difference, it does not make it a level playing field. This means that there are also those who will find it difficult to get into employment and who may become NEETs, although here a greater difference could be made and there are case studies in this book showing some of the innovative ways that are being found to ensure that fewer students with special needs become NEETs.

These issues affect a lot of people, with one in five being identified with SEND and 2.8% with more complex needs.

The attention being given to this sizeable group of learners is to be welcomed and should result in better outcomes for them and a happier experience for them and their families.

The next chapter covers how the system is changing and looks at the work of the SEND Pathfinder authorities in piloting some of the changes. It gives further information on the cultural shift the 2015 SEND Code of Practice represents and leads into the final chapter in Part One of this book, which is devoted to an overview of the SEND Code.

Further reading

For additional information, you can refer to the relevant sections of the SEND Code of Practice 2015:
SEND Code of Practice (2015): Foreword and Introduction.

DCSF (2009) *Lamb Inquiry: Special Educational Needs and Parental Confidence.* Nottingham: DCSF Publications.

DfES (2011b) *Special Educational Needs: Code of Practice.* Nottingham: DfES Publications.

Ofsted (2010) *The Special Educational Needs and Disability Review: A Statement is Not Enough.* Manchester: Ofsted Publications.

Tutt, R. (2007) *Every Child Included.* London: Paul Chapman Publishing.

2

The implications of the Children and Families Act (2014)

Chapter overview

Following on from the previous chapter's description of the lead up to the changes and why change was felt to be necessary, this chapter sets out the steps that resulted in a new SEN Framework being put in place, including a new SEND Code of Practice. It describes:

- The Green Paper that led to the Children and Families Bill
- The content of the Children and Families Act
- The Regulations that go with it
- The work of the SEND Pathfinders.

The chapter ends by explaining how the separate changes add up to a significant shift in culture, particularly in the way professionals work with children and young people and their families.

The start of a change in policy

The previous chapter mentioned that much had been done during Labour's term in office to highlight issues around children and young people with SEND and to look at ways of improving the system. When the Coalition Government took office in May 2010, it was able to build on this work and on the work the Conservatives had done in preparation while in opposition, to look at the whole of the SEND framework, which everyone agreed was ready for its first major overhaul for over 30 years.

The first inkling that major changes were afoot became apparent when Sarah Teather, as Minister for SEN, launched the *Green Paper: Children and Young People With Special Educational Needs and Disabilities – Call for Views* (DfE, 2010a), in the autumn of 2010.

Key point: The making of an Act

Green Papers are preliminary consultation documents the government produces when it is thinking of introducing a new law. It allows people both inside and outside Parliament to give their views on any proposals that are being put forward. They may lead on to a White Paper being produced with firmer proposals, or to a Bill.

White Papers are produced when a government has fairly clear ideas of the policy changes it wants to enact, but may still want to invite comments, before putting the ideas forward in a Bill.

Bills usually stem from a White (or Green) Paper and once they have been debated in both Houses of Parliament, they receive Royal Assent and become **Acts** and pass into law.

The Call for Views attracted a great deal of interest, although, as Sarah Teather mentioned at the time, respondents were better at defining the problems with the current system than suggesting solutions.

The SEND Green Paper

A few months later, in March 2011, a more solid consultation document appeared entitled: *Support and Aspiration: A New Approach to SEND* (DfE, 2011a). This clarified the government's thinking and some key issues emerged. Teather had spent a considerable amount of time talking to parents, in groups and as individuals, and she knew their frustrations in terms of not having enough say in what happened to their children; having to repeat their story over and over again to different professionals who appeared to work in isolation; and not being able to find the information they needed about the support available for their children and the family as a whole. So, a central tenet of the new Framework was the idea of placing children, young people and their families at the centre of the decisions that affect them. The Green Paper also established the SEND Pathfinders, to try out some of the new ways of working. These are described in more detail later in this chapter.

For over a year, all seemed to go quiet. The Pathfinders took time to establish themselves and, to begin with, had little impact beyond those who were directly involved. Following this seeming hiatus, three events happened in quick succession. There was a mention in the Queen's Speech when she opened Parliament (May 2012) of a Children and Families Bill, which provided the legislative context for the changes; a follow-up document to the Green Paper: *Support and Aspiration: A New Approach to Special Educational Needs and Disability – Progress and Next Steps* (DfE 2012) appeared; and a government reshuffle led to Sarah Teather being replaced as Minister with responsibility for SEN by Edward Timpson. So, all of a sudden, the SEND agenda started gathering momentum again.

Children and Families Bill

The Bill went much wider than SEN and, like other recent Bills, was composed of several separate parts which did not necessarily hang together, but were pieces of legislation the government wished to push through. By far the largest part, and the one that aroused the most interest, was Part 3 on Special Educational Needs. Below is a list of all the parts of the Bill:

1. Adoption and Children Looked After by LAs
2. Family Justice
3. Children & Young People with SEN
4. Childminder Agencies
5. The Children's Commissioner
6. Statutory Rights to Leave and Pay
7. Time Off Work
8. Right to Request Flexible Working.

While some of these other parts are also relevant to schools and other settings, this book is concerned with Part 3 of the Bill.

The Bill was very thoroughly discussed by both the House of Commons and the House of Lords and many amendments were suggested, including some to do with disability.

Since the SEN and Disability Act 2001 (which was mentioned in the last chapter), people had become used to referring to SEN and disability, and it was a surprise when Part 3 of the Bill only referred to SEN. Due to the amendments that were put forward, disability was threaded into some parts of the Act and the heading of Part 3 was adjusted to reflect this, so it now refers to children and young people with SEN *or disabilities*. However, the overlap between these two terms, one originating from education and one from health, has still not been clearly defined. The Bill took all of 2013 and the first part of 2014 to become an Act.

SEN Regulations (2014)

Regulations are secondary legislation which set out in more detail what the law requires. Once the Bill became the Children and Families Act, the final Regulations were put before Parliament and accepted. The Regulations cover:

- Assessments
- EHC Plans
- Personal budgets
- Mediation
- Appeals
- Miscellaneous provisions
- Special educational needs co-ordinators
- SEN information report (+ Schedule 1*)
- Local Offer (+ Schedule 2 which lists what LAs must cover in their Local Offer)
- Approval of independent special schools and post-16 institutions
- Parents and young people lacking capacity.

[Note: *Schedule 1 gives a list on one page of the items schools must cover when writing the SEN Information Report that goes on their website and which needs updating at least once a year, or more frequently if there are particular changes to what a school provides or how they provide it.]

In 2015, when the SEND Code of Practice was issued, an extra Regulation was published (SEND (Detained Persons) Regulation 2015), to reflect the changes that had been made to the arrangements for those in youth custody, (see Chapter 10 of the 2015 SEND Code of Practice).

The components of the new SEN Framework

Sometimes there is confusion about what exactly is meant by an SEN Framework. So, in a nutshell, there are three parts to it:

1. Part 3 of the Children and Families Act (as listed previously)
2. The Regulations that go alongside the Act (as discussed in the previous paragraphs)
3. The SEND Code of Practice: 0 to 25 years (which is covered in the next chapter).

Over time, case law may be added to this, as the SEN Framework becomes a reality and any difficulties associated with it begin to emerge.

The work of the SEND Pathfinders

From the time the Green Paper was published in March 2011, some of the main elements of the changes to the SEN Framework were piloted by the

SEND Pathfinders. Although the idea was that this would feed into the Bill before it became an Act, the original timetable was too short to enable this to happen. Fortunately, the timetable was extended twice, so that instead of ending in 2013, it ran on to March 2015.

The SEND Pathfinder Programme

The Pathfinder Programme was launched in September 2011. From the LAs who put themselves forward, 31 were selected to form 20 Pathfinders. Some opted to work with other LAs and some on their own, but, in either case, they had to work with their partners in the health service. The pathfinders were selected partly to make sure there was a geographical spread and also to ensure that different LAs were included, from large shire counties and city conurbations to small unitary LAs. The original Pathfinders were:

South East:	SE7*
	Southampton
South West:	Cornwall & Isles of Scilly
	Devon
	Wiltshire
London:	Bexley & Bromley
	Greenwich
	Lewisham
East:	Hertfordshire
E & W Midlands:	Northamptonshire & Leicester City
	Nottinghamshire
	Solihull
North West:	Manchester
	Oldham & Rochdale
	Trafford
	Wigan
North East:	Gateshead
	Hartlepool & Darlington
Yorkshire and Humber:	Calderdale
	North Yorkshire

[Note: *South East 7 consisted of: Brighton and Hove, E. Sussex, Hampshire, Kent, Medway, Surrey and W. Sussex.]

In later phases of the programme, some became Pathfinder champions and took on a regional role, a national role or both, while some chose to include non-Pathfinder LAs as well. (In Chapter 5 of this book, there is a case study of a Pathfinder who took on all these roles).

The thematic areas the Pathfinders piloted were:

- Preparing for adulthood and post 16
- Co-ordinated assessment and single Education, Health and Care Plans
- Personal budgets
- The Local Offer
- Joint commissioning
- Engagement with children, young people and parents/carers
- Participation of education settings for ages 0–25
- Organisational change and workforce development.

As well as contributing to the development of the Bill, all those involved in the Pathfinder programme, had a role in making sure the non-Pathfinder areas were up to speed with the changes. Some of the LAs who had not been involved previously were brought in to work alongside the Pathfinders at a later stage. Although the Pathfinder Programme came to an end in March 2015, for the following year an SEN and disability Peer Network Programme was planned, where an LA or consortia of LAs in each region, would take the lead in driving forward the SEN reforms.

Information Packs

Information Packs covering most of these key areas were published in June 2013 and updated in December 2013, April 2014 and October 2014. They provide a useful overview of the different ways the Pathfinders discovered of implementing the main changes to the SEN Framework.

Activity

Choose a local authority you know and two you are not familiar with and spend time looking at the way they have presented their Local Offer.

- What are the similarities?
- What are the differences?
- Which is easiest to find your way around and why is this?

NB Many LAs will have a separate website for their local offer, but some may not. In either case, they should be easy to find by putting in the name of the LA followed by 'Local Offer'.

The cultural shift from one SEND system to the next

The intention of the reforms is often described as bringing about a cultural change. While it may be comparatively easy to change systems, a change in culture can take longer to achieve, as people have to move on from previous ways of working and embrace a change in practice. The main changes to the SEN system were described briefly in the last chapter and will be explained fully in the next chapter on the SEND Code of Practice 2015. But before explaining what a change of culture means in the context of a new SEN Framework, here is a reminder of the main changes:

- The SEND age range increased to 0–25 years of age
- Local authorities (LAs) to publish a Local Offer describing the services available to children and young people with SEND and their families
- LAs, health and social care to commission jointly the services required for SEND
- Education, health and social care to co-ordinate assessments that may or may not lead to Education, Health and Care Plans (EHC Plans)
- Statements (for under 16-year-olds) and Learning Difficulty Assessments (for over 16-year-olds) to be replaced by EHC Plans for 0–25-year-olds
- Health commissioners to deliver the agreed health elements of the EHC Plan
- Families whose children have an EHC Plan to have the option of a personal budget
- New statutory protections for young people aged 16–25 in Further Education (FE)

So what are these changes trying to achieve?

Children and families at the centre

First and foremost, the changes place children, young people and their families at the centre, so that they feel more in control of a system where many have felt their views were not really considered to be important and decisions were sometimes made by people who had little or no face-to-face contact with them.

To enable this change to happen, much else follows:

- The three key services of education, health and social care need to work together, so that parents do not have to keep retelling their story to different professionals and a more holistic view can be taken of a child's needs.
- The idea of the Local Offer means that all the information to make informed choices will be available in one place.
- Increasing the age range is intended to cut out the problems families often experienced as young people were moved from children's services to adult services and an entirely different set of professionals came into their lives.
- Personal budgets for families have been tried in other services and now the idea is being extended to EHC Plans so that, again, greater control is in the hands of young people and their families and they have more say over how the money is spent.

Further information on all these elements is given in the next chapter on the SEND Code of Practice, and illustrations of how they are working out in practice are included throughout the book.

Multi-agency working

Of course, this is not the first time that there has been a focus on the services for children working more closely together. The *Every Child Matters* (ECM) Green Paper, which led to the Children Act of 2004 followed Lord Laming's Inquiry into the death of Victoria Climbié, (House of Commons Health Committee, The Victoria Climbié Inquiry Report, Sixth Report of Sessions 2002–03). Here was a child who had been known to many professionals in the different services, but they failed to share their knowledge and so the opportunity to build up a picture of the appalling treatment she suffered at the hands of those who were responsible for her welfare was never created and ultimately resulted in her death.

After the Children Act, Local Education Authorities (LEAs) were replaced by Local Authorities (LAs), with many appointing a Director of Children's Services, responsible for both education and social care. So, this time round, attention was focused on tying in health, and many of the documents about the changes to the SEN Framework have been issued jointly by the Department for Education (DfE) and the Department of Health.

The next chapter concentrates on the *SEND Code of Practice: 0 to 25 Years*, which, after many variations and consultations, was published at the end of July 2014. It elaborates on all the main areas of the changes discussed so far, including the implications for early years, schools and post-16 education.

Further reading

For additional information, you can refer to the relevant sections of the SEND Code of Practice 2015:
SEND Code of Practice (2015): Chapter 1 – Principles.

DfE (2011a) *Support and Aspiration: A New Approach to Special Needs and Disability.* London: HMSO.

DfE (2012): *Support and Aspiration: A New Approach to SEND – Progress and Next Steps.* London: HMSO.

DfE (2014a) *Children and Families Act.* London: HMSO.

DfE (2014c) *The Young Person's Guide to the Children and Families Act 2014,* www.gov.uk/government/publications

The SEND Code of Practice: 0–25 years

The development of the SEND Code (2015)

It is not unusual for a Bill to take a considerable time wending its way through Parliament before becoming an Act. It is less common for a Code of Practice to go through several incarnations before the final version appears. While it was clear all along that there would need to be a new SEND Code of Practice to reflect the changes in the Children and Families Act (2014), what could not have been anticipated at the outset was the amount of controversy it would stir up and the length of time it would take to resolve the issues that had been raised. Another unexpected outcome was that the government started out with the stated intention of making the SEND Code shorter than the 2001 version, which had 201 pages. Although the version issued for the first consultation was only 174 pages, by the time the final version appeared, it had grown to 292 pages. As the current Code incorporates all those working with children and young people throughout the extended age range of 0–25, this is not altogether surprising. This chapter traces the stages of the *SEND Code of Practice: 0–25 years* and the changes that were made along the way, before the final version appeared in January 2015.

The draft codes

Most people outside Parliament were unaware of a very early draft of the Code which appeared in March 2013, so that MPs could study it alongside discussions of the Children and Families Bill. What came to public attention was the Draft SEN Code that appeared in October 2013, with a consultation period lasting from 4 October to 9 December. Looking back, it is interesting to note that this one was called *Draft Special Educational Needs (SEN) Code of Practice: For 0–25 Years*. There was no mention of 'disability' as, at that stage, Part 3 of the Bill was headed 'Special Educational Needs', and the later amendments which included disability in parts of the Bill had not been discussed.

The consultation attracted over 700 responses. In its response, the Department for Education (DfE) said that some of the main issues had been around:

- A lack of detail on post-16 arrangements as a result of having one chapter covering early years, schools and post-16 provision
- Parental concerns about the transfer of rights to young people at age 16
- Queries about how the Local Offer and arrangements for joint commissioning would work in practice
- The lack of cross referencing, both between chapters and with other legislation.

The feedback was acted upon and the next version had separate chapters for early years providers, schools and Further Education (FE) (chapters 5, 6 and 7). In addition, a new chapter was added entitled 'Preparing for Adulthood from the Earliest Years' (chapter 8). To address concerns about the right to make decisions being given to young people at the age of 16, 'Annex 1: Mental Capacity' was included. The chapter covering the Local Offer (chapter 4) was extended, and the chapter on 'Working Together across Education, Health and Care' (chapter 3) was expanded to include two paragraphs on joint commissioning arrangements. The whole document was tidied up with more cross-referencing between the chapters and the inclusion at the start of each one of a list of relevant legislation.

As there had been so many changes, it was necessary to hold a second consultation. Another version of the Code was published in April 2014, with a short consultation period running from 16 April to 6 May 2014. This attracted a more favourable response, although a significant number of respondents were still not satisfied. By now, it had become the SEND Code rather than the SEN Code, due to amendments to the Bill mentioned previously. Having to hold a second consultation meant a delay in publishing the SEND Code and making it available for schools and other settings and services.

In June 2014, the Code was laid before Parliament. It was passed at the end of July, after MPs had left for the summer recess and just in time for the House of Lords to agree with the decision already endorsed by MPs, that it should be approved. So, with the addition of a Foreword by Edward Timpson, Parliamentary Under-Secretary of State (and Minister for SEN), and Dr Dan Poulter, his equivalent in the Department of Health, the *Special Educational Needs and Disability Code of Practice: 0 to 25 Years* (July 2014) was in place. However, as explained in the note at the start of the Introductory chapter, this was superceded in January 2015 by the *Special Educational Needs and Disability Code of Practice: 0 to 25 Years*, which came into effect from April 2015.

The main contents of the SEND Code of Practice 2015

The following sections give an outline of the contents of the Code. Some parts are explained in greater detail, either because they have a bearing on the rest of this book, or because they are likely to be of particular interest. There will be further references to the Code and quotes from it in the other chapters. The case studies include examples of reactions to it and how it is being implemented.

Introduction to the SEND Code

The list of who the Code is for shows why it turned into such a lengthy document. It includes:

- Local authorities in the shape of education, social care and relevant housing and employment services
- Governing bodies of schools, including non-maintained special schools, FE colleges and sixth form colleges
- The proprietors of academies (including free schools, University Technical Colleges (UTCs) and Studio Schools)
- The management committees of pupil referral units (PRUs)
- Independent schools and independent specialist providers
- All early years providers funded by LAs, whether from the maintained, private, independent or voluntary sectors
- National Health Service Commissioning Boards, clinical commissioning groups (CCGs), NHS Trusts, NHS Foundation Trusts and Local Health Boards
- Youth Offending Teams and relevant custodial establishments
- The First-tier Tribunal (Special Educational Needs and Disability).

From this, it is apparent how this Code is having to take in a much wider audience, due to the inclusion of post-16 to 25 provision, the proliferation of different types of educational settings since the previous Code, and the efforts being made to tie in those working in the Health Service. For those who were used to working with the 2001 SEN Code of Practice, the Introduction also has a very useful summary of the main changes:

- The extension of the age range to 25 years
- The inclusion of disabled children and young people
- Children, young people and their families being far more closely involved at both individual and strategic levels
- The emphasis on the outcomes families want
- The need for joint planning and commissioning between education, health and social care
- The establishment of a Local Offer of support for young people with SEND and their families
- A graduated approach to identifying and supporting pupils with SEND
- A co-ordinated approach to assessment and Education Health and Care Plans
- A carefully planned transition to adulthood.

The Introduction clarifies that the 2015 Code replaces: the 2001 Code; Inclusive Schooling (2001); and the Statutory Guidance on Learning Difficulty Assessments, which, along with statements, are being replaced by EHC Plans. Mention is also made of the inclusion of the relevant duties under the Equality Act (DfE, 2010b) and the relevant provisions of the Mental Capacity Act (DCSF, 2005).

Key point: Equality Act 2010 🔑

Schools, early years providers, post-16 institutions and LAs (among others) have a legal obligation to:

- Not discriminate, harass or victimise children and young people who are disabled
- Make reasonable adjustments so that they are not at a substantial disadvantage compared with their peers, including providing auxiliary aids and services. This includes planning for future requirements
- Have regard to the need to eliminate discrimination, promote equality of opportunity, and foster good relations between disabled and non-disabled children and young people
- Publish information showing how they are complying and have objectives to achieve these core aims.

While the Equality Act is usually familiar to people working in educational settings, the Mental Capacity Act may be less well known. For this reason, 'Annex 1: Mental Capacity' explains in some detail what it covers and why it is important in the context of SEND. Finally, the definitions of SEN and of disability are set out, although they have not changed since the 2001 Code of Practice.

Chapter 1: Principles

Part 3 of the Children and Families Act begins by setting out the principles that underpin the reforms, and they are repeated at the beginning of the first chapter of the Code. These state that LAs must have regard to:

- The views, wishes and feelings of the child or young person and their parents
- The importance of involving them in decisions and being given the information to enable them to participate as fully as possible
- The support needed by the child or young person and their parents, in order to help achieve the best possible educational and other outcomes, to prepare them for adulthood.

The Code introduces the Parent Carer Forums, which, since 2011, have had a national structure in the form of the National Network of Parent Carer Forums (NNPCF).

Some Parent Carer Forums were used by the SEND Pathfinders as one of the ways of gathering the views of groups of parents and carers.

Key point: National Network of Parent Carer Forums 🔑

The NNPCF was launched, with government funding, in 2011, to bring together the 150 local Parent Carer Forums that exist in almost every LA area. The Forums are arranged into nine regions: NE and Cumbria; Yorks and Humberside; NW; E. Midlands; W. Midlands; Eastern England; London; South West; and South East.

Over 52,000 parents belong to the Forums and each Forum includes parent carers with experience of health, education and social care. The NNPCF works closely with LAs and Health Authorities at all levels, including clinical commissioning groups (CCGs).

Website: www.nnpcf.org.uk

The chapter includes: LAs' duty to identify all children and young people who have, or may have, SEND (with the health service bringing to the LA's attention any child under compulsory school age); how families will be given more choice and control; how the services will support them by working together; what high-quality provision and inclusive practice look like; and what is meant by a successful preparation for adulthood. These are key themes that run throughout the Code and are elaborated on in the succeeding chapters.

Chapter 2: Impartial information, advice and support

This chapter focuses on the information LAs should make available to children, young people and their parents, much of which will be contained in their Local Offer (see chapter 4 of the Code). It mentions the work of Parent Partnership Services (PPS), who, since the Code was written, have become Information, Advice and Support Services. The chapter also mentions the Independent Supporters who have been trained to provide further support to families in finding their way through the changes to the system.

Key point: Parent Partnership Services and Independent Supporters O━

Parent Partnership Services (PPS)/Information, Advice and Support Services (IASS) were established in LAs to support parents and carers of children and young people with SEN. In 2014, their name was changed from PPS to Information, Advice and Support Services.

Independent Supporters

In January 2014, the DfE announced a new £30 million fund to train 1,800 Independent Supporters to help parents understand the new SEN system. These people come from voluntary, community and private organisations and help guide families through the new way of assessing pupils and the EHC Plan process

---

LAs and IASS will work together to help identify families most in need of support.

The chapter stresses that LAs should adopt a key working approach, so families have a single point of contact.

Chapter 3: Working together across education, health and care for joint outcomes

The Children and Families Act went through Parliament at much the same time as the Care Act 2014, and there are important links between them. For instance, the Care Act requires LAs to ensure that there is co-operation between children's and adults' services, so that there is a continuation of care. It explains the joint commissioning requirements which involve health as well, both for those with and without an EHC Plan.

On page 43 of the Code, paragraph 3.20, there is a diagram showing the relationship between Health and Wellbeing Boards, joint commissioning arrangements, the Local Offer and EHC Plans. Below is an adaptation of the information contained in paragraph 3.20 of the Code.

Health and Wellbeing Boards look at the needs of the whole population and develop a **Joint Strategic Needs Assessment** (JSNA), which includes an analysis of vulnerable groups, one of which is the SEND population.

The information in the JSNA is then used by the LA and CCGs to inform the *joint commissioning* decisions for SEND and agree outcomes with children, young people and their families, e.g. through the Parent Carer Forums.

The LA's **Local Offer** reflects the services needed, as identified in the JSNA, and publishes the support available to 0–25-year-olds with SEND.

At the individual level, services co-operate to arrange the provision agreed in the **EHC Plan**, which, in turn, informs the JSNA process.

The rest of chapter 3 of the Code covers joint planning and commissioning including in the context of EHC Plans and personal budgets. Both of these are covered more fully in chapter 9 of the Code.

Chapter 4: The Local Offer

The quote from paragraph 4.1 of the chapter sums up what the Local Offer means:

> Local authorities **must** publish a Local Offer, setting out in one place information about provision they expect to be available across education, health and social care for children and young people in their area who have SEN or are disabled, including those who do not have an Education, Health and Care plan. (DfE/DoH, 2014a: 59)

In the run up to the changes, there was some confusion about the Local Offer, and the term the 'School's Offer' was bandied about. As chapter 4 of the Code makes clear, compiling the Local Offer is an LA's responsibility, but schools, as well as other education settings and services, must co-operate with the LA by linking their websites to the Local Offer. The responsibility for making sure this happens lies with the governing bodies of maintained schools, sixth form colleges and FE colleges; the proprietors of academies, free schools and non-maintained special schools; and the management committees of pupil referral units (PRUs). The task is being tackled differently in different LAs and some of the case studies in this book give examples of how this new responsibility is being handled.

Chapter 4 of the Code also explains that the LA must invite feedback, particularly from children, young people and their families, on the Local Offer and must report how they have addressed any comments they receive. In this way it is hoped that the Local Offers will be of growing value, both for the information they contain and as a means of moving forward the provision for learners with SEND.

Chapter 5: Early years providers

This is the first of the three chapters which enlarged on chapter 6 in the October 2013 draft, in order to give due weight to the importance of early years providers and post-16 provision (chapter 7). It covers:

- Early identification from 0 to 2 years and the Progress Check at 2
- The link with the early years foundation stage (EYFS) and the EYFS Profile
- The four broad categories of need (with social, emotional and mental health difficulties replacing BESD)
- How to deliver SEN support using the Assess – Plan – Do – Review cycle
- The role of the SENCO and Area SENCOs in early years provision.

The Code stresses the need to be alert to any emerging difficulties young children may have, to put in place the support they need and to work in close partnership with parents.

Chapter 6: Schools

One of the differences between this Code and the 2001 Code is the greater attention given to pupils with medical conditions, and where they also have SEN, the need to co-ordinate their healthcare plans with the provision put in place to support their educational needs. There is a reference to the guidance, *Supporting Pupils at School with Medical Conditions* (DfE 2014d), which the DfE published in April 2014, with another version in June 2014.

As mentioned earlier, the four broad categories of need are the same as in the previous Code, apart from social, emotional and mental health difficulties replacing BESD. A further explanation about this change and the views of schools about the change is given in some of the case study material.

The graduated approach to support is specified in terms of: Assess – Plan – Do – Review. This replaced the stages of School Action and School Action Plus in the previous Code. Again, there are comments on the disappearance of the previous staged approach later on in this book. Although there is no requirement for a particular type of record keeping, such as an Individual Education Plan (IEP), the importance of keeping records and working closely with parents is stressed. The requirement for schools to publish an SEN Information Report and what it should contain is set out in paragraph 6.79. As mentioned before, there has been some confusion about this and schools are tackling it in different ways. The fact that the SEN Information Report must be published at least annually and the points it has to cover are quite clear. What is less clear is its relationship with the school's contribution to the Local Offer and the school's SEN Policy, on which there is very little guidance. Again, this will be discussed further in connection with some of the case studies (see pages 108–9).

The need for every teacher, whether a class teacher, a subject teacher or a teacher working in another capacity, to see themselves as a teacher of every pupil in their class or classes is a central feature of the new SEN system. In tandem with this is the strategic role played by SENCOs and their roles and responsibilities are considered at some length (see paragraphs 6.84–6.94).

Chapter 7: Further Education

The final chapter for educational settings is new to the Code, as FE Colleges and other forms of post-16 provision are included in the Code for the first time. There was some discussion while the Bill was going through Parliament about including Higher Education (HE) as well, and some disappointment that amendments put through on the subject were not passed. As SEND goes up to the age of 25, this might be seen as a missed opportunity.

Although FE Colleges are included, the requirements are less stringent than they are for schools. For instance, although providers must 'use their best endeavours' to provide the necessary support to students with SEND, how this is achieved is left to the providers. Although there should be a named person in the college with oversight of SEN provision, this is not the same as the role of a SENCO.

Chapter 8: Preparing for adulthood from the earliest years

This is a new chapter that was added as a result of the first consultation. 'From the earliest years' is a reference to the need for students and their families to be aspirational and to have long-term goals, where most of them will continue to study after school, hold down a job and become as independent as possible. There are sections on:

- Planning transition from Year 9 onwards, with 'Preparing for adulthood' reviews (for those with an EHC Plan)
- 16–17-year-olds
- 19–25-year-olds
- Planning the transition to post-16 education and training, and to HE where appropriate
- Careers advice and pathways to employment

This is a chapter devoted to making smoother transitions between the stages of a young person's life and to considering the implications of the extended age range to 25 years.

Chapter 9: Education, Health and Care needs assessments and Plans

In the same way that a formal assessment might have led to a statement, a statutory assessment may lead to an EHC Plan. These have to be completed within a tighter timescale than under the statementing procedures. They must:

- Take into account the views, interests and aspirations of the child and their family
- Take on board the information obtained from the assessment, including advice from the school, the educational psychologist (EP), social care and health
- Consider how best to achieve the outcomes sought for the child or young person, including the special educational provision to be made towards those outcomes
- Identify any elements of support to be secured by a personal budget.

Key point: Personal budgets

A personal budget is for the *additional* support the child or family may need. It is optional, but LAs must prepare a budget if requested to do so, in which case, the details will be set out as part of an EHC Plan. Parents will be able to choose:

- whether they wish the LA, or a third party, to manage the funds on their behalf
- whether they would like a **direct payment** and commission services themselves.

Where there is a direct payment, the LA must secure the agreement of the early years setting, school or college regarding how the direct payment is to be spent.

Initially, there were many concerns about what would happen if a family's views on the support they wanted clashed with the school, but there are safeguards to ensure that agreement is reached at the stage the Plan is being drawn up, to prevent this from happening.

When the pathfinders began piloting EHC Plans, they had a great deal of freedom to decide how the contents were set out. In view of the variability this produced, and the difficulty in being able to see at a glance whether or not they met legal requirements, the Code and the Regulations set out the sections that must be included as a minimum. These are as follows:

Content of EHC Plan (summarised from page 161, paragraph 9.62 of the SEND Code of Practice 2014)

Section A	The views, interests and aspirations of the child and his or her parents
Section B	His or her special educational needs
Section C	Any health needs that are related to their SEN
Section D	Any social care needs that are related to their SEN or disability
Section E	How shorter-term targets will be set and the longer-term outcomes sought, including outcomes for adult life
Section F	The special educational provision required
Section G	Any health provision needed because of their learning difficulties or disabilities, which result in their having SEN. If they have an Individual Health Care Plan (IHCP), that should be included
Section H1	If they are under 18, any social care provision they are entitled to under section 2 of the Chronically Sick and Disabled Person's Act 1970
Section H2	Any other social care provision reasonably required because of their learning difficulties or disabilities, which result in their having SEN, including any adult social care provision for which they are eligible under the Care Act 2014
Section I	The name and type of provision to be attended
Section J	The details of any personal budget, how it will be used to support the outcomes, the provision it will be used for, and the arrangements for any direct payments for education, health and social care
Section K	The advice and information from the EHC needs assessment must be included as appendices.

If a young person is in or past Year 9, sections F, G, H1 or H2 (as appropriate) must include the provision required to assist in preparing for adulthood and independent living.

Chapter 10: Children and young people in specific circumstances

This chapter contains most of the differences between the July 2014 SEND Code and the one that was issued in January 2015. It covers children and young people, who, as well as having SEN, come under one of the categories listed:

- Looked after children (LAC) and young people leaving the care system
- Children and young people with SEN and social care needs, including children in need
- Children and young people educated out of area
- Children and young people with SEN educated at home
- Children and young people in alternative provision
- Children and young people who have SEN and are in hospital
- Children of service personnel
- Children and young people in youth custody.

There are paragraphs on each of these specific circumstances, but the message is to ensure that a holistic view is taken, so that when planning the support a child or young person needs, other factors apart from SEND are taken into account. Those in custody were a late addition to the Children and Families 2014 Act. through an amendment. This was much needed because of the high proportion of those who are detained, or find themselves in prison, who have unidentified or unmet special needs.

Chapter 11: Resolving disagreements

The final chapter of the Code considers what LAs must put in place to try to settle any disputes there may be with parents before they consider going to the SEND Tribunal. Originally, the government had hoped to make mediation compulsory, but this was rejected. Nevertheless, it has to be made available and offered to families, who have to consider mediation before going to Tribunal. Although, as the Code points out, the terms 'disagreement resolution' and 'mediation' are often used interchangeably, the Act gives different meanings to these two terms.

Key point: Resolving disputes 🔑

Disagreement resolution services LAs must make these available, although their use is voluntary. The services are commissioned by LAs, but must be independent. They may be used at any time to sort out disputes early on. Families can also use the Independent Supporters in this capacity.

Continued

Continued

Mediation   If disputes cannot be settled in this way, the next layer before the Tribunal system is mediation. The mediation arrangements only cover decisions about an EHC needs assessment or an EHC Plan, whereas the disagreement resolution service is much wider in scope.

SEND Tribunal   Officially called the First-tier Tribunal (SEN and disability), it deals with complaints from young people or their parents about an LA's decision not to assess a child, not to issue an EHCP, or some of the wording in the Plan.

As well as the chapters already mentioned, the final version of the SEND Code 2015 has two Annexes

Annex 1: Mental capacity

This explains what happens if young people over 16, or their parents, do not have the mental capacity to be involved in making decisions. The four key questions are:

- Can the person understand information, including the consequences of making, or not making the decision?
- Can they retain this information for long enough to make the decision?
- Can they use and weigh the information to arrive at a choice?
- Can they communicate their decision in any way?

Annex 2: Improving practice and staff training in education settings

While early years providers, schools and colleges are responsible for making the decision about when to call on outside specialists and for their priorities in terms of the professional development of their staff, the Annex suggests that support is delivered most effectively where there is a structured approach to:

- Engaging parents and children
- Tracking and measuring progress
- Ensuring a good level of knowledge across all staff of different types of SEN and suitable teaching approaches and interventions.

The Annex provides links to a number of organisations offering support and training to schools on identification and teaching approaches for pupils with SEN as well as on specific conditions. Some of these will be referred to in Chapter 9 of this book, which is about workforce development.

Where a setting has a SENCO, they should play an important part in advising on and contributing to the broader support provided by schools and the professional development of other teachers and staff. (Annex 2, SEND Code of Practice 2015)

Having considered the contents of the Code, the rest of the book looks at the context for its implementation and how it is impacting on provision and practice through a range of case studies of different settings.

Further reading

For additional information, you can refer to the relevant sections of the SEND Code of Practice 2015:
SEND Code of Practice (2015): Chapter 2 – Impartial Information, Advice and Support.

DfE/DoH (2014a) *Special Educational Needs and Disability Code of Practice: 0 to 25 Years.* www.gov.uk/government/publications

DfE (2014f) *Early Years: Guide to the 0–25 SEND Code of Practice.* Department for Education.

DfE (2014g) *Further Education: Guide to the 0–25 SEND Code of Practice.* Department for Education.

DfE (2014h) *Schools: Guide to the 0–25 SEND Code of Practice.* Department for Education.

PART TWO

PROVISION

Newer patterns of provision for pupils with SEN

Chapter overview

This is the first of three chapters looking at how the pattern of provision for pupils with SEND is changing across all types of schools. It considers how this is leading to a more flexible and inclusive continuum of provision. This is encouraged by the emphasis in the SEND Code of Practice 2015 on (i) greater choice for families and (ii) all teachers seeing themselves as teachers of young learners who have special needs.

   After clarifying how the term 'provision' is being used, there are case studies to illustrate how primary, secondary and special schools are meeting a wider range of needs, by adapting the environment to make it more inclusive, adjusting what is on offer for the pupils and taking steps to improve the knowledge and skills of staff.

Provision for learners with SEND

The word 'provision' can be used in different ways. In *Planning and Developing Special Educational Provision: A Guide for Local Authorities and other Proposers* (DCSF, 2007), which was mentioned in Chapter 1 of this book, it is used to refer to the different types of provision that local authorities (LAs) and other providers may have in terms of schools and other educational settings for children and young people with special educational needs (SEN). This is the way it is used in Part Two of this book, which considers the growing range of provision for children and young people with SEND, including what is becoming available for them up to the age of 25 years. On the other hand, when the word 'provision' is used within the context of 'special educational *provision*', it often refers to the kinds of support and interventions that an educational setting may employ to address the needs of its learners. This is the sense in which it is used in Part Three of this book and in chapter 6 of the SEND Code of Practice 2014, where paragraphs 6.36 to 6.43 are headed 'Special educational provision in schools'.

In the first of the three chapters on provision, the focus is on how primary, secondary and special schools are finding ways of creating environments that support the inclusion of a wider range of pupils. The Guidance mentioned in the previous paragraph was developed as a result of Andrew Adonis (Lord Adonis), who was Minister for SEN at the time, encouraging LAs to maintain 'a flexible continuum of provision' and clarifying what this might look like. The Guidance lists the following as possible types of provision:

- Mainstream schools
- Mainstream schools with an SEN specialism in one of the four areas of need in the Code of Practice
- Mainstream schools with Resourced Provision for specific types of need, where pupils are mainly taught in mainstream classes, but have access to a base or specialist facilities
- Mainstream schools with a Designated Unit, where pupils are taught wholly or mainly in separate classes
- Special schools for particular types of SEN
- Special schools with an SEN specialism in one of the four areas of need
- Co-location, where special and mainstream schools share a site and there is some interchange of pupils, resources and staff
- Co-location, where a special school shares a site with a provider other than a mainstream school
- Special schools with Resourced Provision or Designated Units for a subset of pupils within the school.

The 2007 Guidance helped to shift the focus from seeing schools in terms of two separate types of provision – mainstream and special – to taking the more pragmatic view, that as learners with SEN cover a huge range in terms of the degree and complexity of their needs, it is important to have a continuum of provision to match their varying and changing needs.

Since Adonis issued his guidance to LAs, there have been two significant changes. Firstly, the amount of specialist provision across the continuum has continued to grow, with both the Specialist Schools Programme and Building Schools for the Future (BSF), being two key drivers. Although receiving specialist school status through a separate programme came to an end in April 2011, mainstream and special schools continue to be recognised for their expertise in one of the four broad areas of need in the 2001 SEN Code of Practice, as well as for curriculum specialisms. The BSF programme, as such, has also ended, but had a lasting impact on using the opportunity when new schools needed to be built, of co-locating mainstream and special schools. (Since BSF, some good or outstanding schools have been able to expand through the Targeted Basic Need Programme, while the Priority School Building Programme has helped some of the schools in urgent need of repair or a complete rebuild.)

Children and young people with complex needs

While it is possible to argue about the various reasons *why* the school population has become more complex, most people working in schools and other educational settings today, would probably agree that they are seeing more pupils who have very significant barriers to their learning. Since the SEN Code of Practice was published in 2001, there have been many changes to the pupil population. These include:

- A significant increase in children being diagnosed with autism
- Newer conditions such as foetal alcohol spectrum disorder (FASD) and pathological demand avoidance syndrome (PDA) being recognised
- More rare syndromes being identified, each one rare in itself, but the total number of rare syndromes is increasing
- Children and young people being more likely to survive life-threatening illnesses or serious accidents
- More babies being born increasingly prematurely and before the development of the brain that normally takes place in the womb has been completed
- A recognition that children and young people may have co-existing conditions, an example being the number diagnosed with both attention deficit hyperactivity disorder (ADHD) and autism.

Medical conditions

The presence in all types of schools of an increasing number of pupils with medical conditions is the reason why the Department for Education (DfE) considered it necessary to issue new statutory guidance to schools, *Supporting Pupils at School with Medical Conditions* (DfE, 2014d), which brought in a new duty for governing bodies of schools to make arrangements to support these pupils. The new duty had to be implemented from September 2014, the same time as the implementation of the Children and Families Act (DfE, 2014a), and, with it, the SEND Code of Practice 2015. The guidance points out that schools need to be aware that some children and young people who have medical conditions may also be disabled and come under the Equality Act (DfE, 2010b) or have SEN, in which case the guidance needs to be read alongside the SEND Code of Practice.

In the new SEND Code, medical needs are given a higher priority. In chapter 5 for early years providers, there is a reminder in paragraph 5.11 that children with medical conditions should get the support they need, as set out in the curriculum for the Early Years Foundation Stage (EYFS). In chapter 6 of the Code, which is the main one for schools, paragraph 6.11 has a reminder that, as a result of the 2014 Act, there is a duty on schools to support pupils with medical conditions and that, in the case of pupils with SEN, an Individual Healthcare Plan (IHCP) should be agreed between the school, the parent and an appropriate healthcare professional. It states that the IHCP should be planned in a co-ordinated way, which means taking into consideration any special needs the child may have.

The fact that new medical guidance was thought to be necessary is further evidence that pupils with complex medical conditions are now being educated in schools of all kinds and not just in special schools.

Activity

1. Discuss with colleagues the overlap between SEN, disability and medical conditions.
2. Look at Annex A of *Supporting Pupils at School with Medical Conditions* (DfE, 2014d), which provides a model process for developing IHCPs and also accompanying templates.
3. If it would be helpful, personalise them for your own setting.

The effort schools have made to address this growing range of needs and its complexities can be shown in the way schools have adapted their provision, or if lucky enough to be able to plan it from scratch, have built features in that recognise a wider range of needs. Mainstream schools, for instance, have some of the facilities that used to be a feature of special schools, which makes sense as their populations are likely to include many children who might previously have attended a special school, while special schools continue to be in demand because of this changing pupil profile.

A primary school case study

The first case study in this chapter is about a primary school that was completely rebuilt a few years ago. The architects worked closely with the school to incorporate features that the staff felt to be important, particularly given a higher than average number of pupils with special needs.

Case study

Water Hall Primary School

Water Hall in Bletchley, near Milton Keynes, is a larger than average primary school, with over 300 3–11-year-olds on roll. The school moved to its current site in 2008. Through an archway bearing the school's name, there are two reception areas, one for the school and one for parents and other members of the community to access their own accommodation without disturbing the rest of the school. Beyond this, a path weaves through a garden area with trees, a mini Stonehenge and seating, before the classrooms are reached

The building is circular and inside the wide corridor, there are alcoves where individual children, or members of staff with one or more pupils, can find a quiet space to work. In addition, there are several extra rooms, including a storytelling room, a room for those needing extra maths, and a spacious library where phonics groups are taught. There are two sensory spaces. The first is a kaleidoscope space, which uses colour and light to create a calming environment to promote well-being. The second is a 4D space, where pupils can be immersed in different environments by means of large-scale corner projection, LED lighting, surround sound and an interactive floor. Operated from a tablet device and wireless switches, pupils can control the different experiences and teachers can use the area for curriculum-based activities, as scenes from the arctic to the desert are displayed on the floor or around the walls.

In the same way that some smaller primary schools have mixed-age classes out of necessity, Water Hall has a similar situation with its published admission number (PAN) of 45 children. The school looks at each cohort and decides how best to meet the children's needs. Having a more flexible approach to placing children in classes can be particularly helpful to some of the pupils with special needs. The school prefers to use the wider term 'targeted children' to cover SEND and other pupils who need additional support or attention. There is a clear identification, assessment and support process for these pupils, who join appropriate one to one or small group intervention programmes. All staff are responsible for monitoring pupil progress and evaluating the effectiveness of interventions.

Some of the Year 6 pupils are very appreciative of the environment for learning they have now and have written about their former school, where they remember: '... the disgusting toilets which smelt really bad; the broken windows which made the classrooms unbearably cold; the holes in the roof which meant that buckets had to be placed to catch the leaks and the stairs which felt unsafe'. The improved surroundings may well have helped the school to move from satisfactory to outstanding. As the SENCO remarked, 'Children need to be in the right place to learn'.

The head teacher, Tony Draper, who oversaw the move from the previous site to its current location is quite clear about the impact the environment makes on the children. In addition, he has been very aware of the changes resulting from the new SEND Framework. The appointment of a family support worker has improved attendance as well as helping to bring school and home closer together. Parents feel welcomed as partners in their children's education and having a Parents' Room has helped even the more reluctant ones to come in to school and feel part of the school community.

Not every school can have the facilities they know would improve pupils' learning, but it may be possible to change the way classes are organised, or how additional support is delivered and to listen to pupils' views about what helps them to learn. Involving parents more closely and helping pupils to contribute their ideas as well, are fundamental to the change in culture envisaged by the SEND Code of Practice.

Resourced provision, units and bases

In most areas, there will be a number of schools that are either resourced to provide for a particular need, such as being accessible to pupils with physical disabilities, or there will be discrete provision which is often described as a unit or base. In secondary schools, there may be a separate department or learning support unit, where pupils can receive additional help for part of the school day. The growth in this kind of facility provides a useful bridge in the continuum of provision between in-class support in a mainstream class and being educated in a special school. One type of unit is often for pupils who are hearing impaired, as this is a low incidence need.

Hearing impairment (HI)

Since 2006, all babies have been screened during the first few weeks of life, to see if they have any degree of hearing loss. This has made it easier to intervene early and find ways of supporting the early stages of language development. Very young children can be fitted with hearing aids or receive cochlear implants, although the latter will not be suitable for every young child with a hearing impairment. It is thought that at least one in every 900 babies born in the UK will have a hearing impairment affecting their language and social development. This figure increases significantly in babies who are born very prematurely. A small minority will be described as profoundly deaf, which means that signing may be their main way of communicating. In addition to having a traditional hearing aid or cochlear implant, pupils may use radio aids. Some schools have invested in a soundfield system, which can help all children to hear more easily and improves their concentration. (This is similar to adults preferring to have some form of amplification, for instance when listening to a speech, even when it is not strictly necessary.)

Key point: Hearing impairment (HI)

Radio aids   This involves the teacher wearing a transmitter, while the pupil wears the receiver attached to their hearing aids or cochlear implant.

Cochlear implants   These are small, surgically implanted electronic devices, with an external part near the ear.

Soundfield systems   The teacher wears a microphone linked to an amplifier. Loudspeakers are placed round the classroom. Some systems are portable, while others are fixed.

The second case study in this chapter is of a primary school in St Albans with an HI Unit. The county has two Units in mainstream schools and two schools for pupils who are hearing impaired or profoundly deaf.

Case study

Maple Primary School

Maple has 220 pupils aged 4–11 years. There are seven classes and the HI Unit, which can accommodate up to nine pupils covering the same age range as the rest of the school. The Unit is staffed by a teacher of the deaf, another part-time teacher and three teaching assistants (TAs). It is equipped with acoustic tiles, double glazing, low frequency emitting lights, rubber soled chairs and soft materials, in order to cut down on extraneous noise. The approach is auditory/aural, meaning that pupils are encouraged to use the hearing that they have and to learn to communicate through speech. Pupils are placed in the Unit after being assessed by the LA as having the potential to develop speech and language without needing to sign. All the HI pupils have a statement or an Education, Health and Care Plan (EHC Plan).

Children in the Unit are full members of one of the other classes, so they can benefit from both settings. They wear post-aural (behind the ear) hearing aids or have cochlear implants. Radio aids are used when they are joining one of the main classes. There are soundfield systems in every classroom and in the hall. When in the Unit, pupils are taught by a teacher of the deaf, who works closely with the rest of the staff to ensure that every pupil has full access to the National Curriculum and to other activities. Each pupil has a personal timetable which includes: individual and small group work in the Unit and time with the speech and language therapist, as well as sessions in the main classes.

The head teacher, Tim Bowen, explains that, in his school, inclusion means that all children are included in the full range of activities that the school has to offer. For some children this may mean doing similar but different activities, or receiving extra support to enable them to participate fully in the same activities as their peers. The school takes the same approach to pupils who are physically disabled. There are ramps for wheelchair users and toilet facilities suitable for both adult and pupil wheelchair users.

Parents are encouraged to be part of the school community and to help supervise activities, accompany class visits, help out with keeping equipment in a good state of repair and maintaining the outside environment. The PTA organises several events each term, including Family Fun Days, discos, film nights, cake sales, uniform sales, the Maple Marathon – a 26-mile walk – and a Dash for Cash.

Tim Bowen says that having pupils who are hearing impaired in the school works both ways. The pupils with HI benefit from specialist teaching and being able to mix with hearing children. The latter, on the other hand, benefit from gaining an understanding of disability and that first and fore-most these are children like themselves, who need support to operate in a hearing world. To make sure all his staff and governors are up to speed with the changes to the SEND Code of Practice, Tim has put training in place for all staff and governors.

Different ways of including pupils with SEND

The first two case studies in this chapter were examples of the different ways in which pupils with SEND can be included. Water Hall has no sepa-rate provision, but makes sure all vulnerable pupils, including those with SEND, receive the support they need and that all pupils can access both indoor and outdoor provision which is designed to improve their sense of well-being. Maple has an HI Unit for those who would struggle to cope full-time in mainstream classes, but are able to be fully included in the school community by having access to the specialist provision within the school. Although this particular provision is not new, the growth in the number of units for different types of needs, reflects a growing understand-ing of how children's learning is affected by whether or not they are in an environment where they feel comfortable and where they have the sup-port they need to enter fully into the life of their school community.

A secondary school case study

The next case study is of a secondary school in London, which chose to become an academy in 2011. It is a stand-alone converter academy, not part of a chain. (Descriptions of different types of academies are given in the next chapter of this book.) A new sixth-form building opened in September 2014. The school is a senior partner in Challenge Partners (see Chapter 9).

Case study

Lampton School in Hounslow

Lampton is a mixed 11–19 comprehensive school of over 1,300 pupils. Four-fifths of its pupils are from minority ethnic groups. One of the school's key principles for inclusion is seeing SEN as a whole-school responsibility, requiring a whole-school response, with every teacher being a teacher of pupils with SEN. So the idea emphasised in the Code of Practice is part and parcel of how the school has been operating for some time.

The Lampton Inclusion Team is led by David Bartram, whose work was mentioned in the Green Paper, *Support and Aspiration: A New Approach to Special Needs and Disability* (DfE, 2011a; see Chapter 1 of this book). As well as supporting pupils in Lampton, David and his team have worked with over 60 other schools across London to raise the attainment of pupils with special needs.

The school has developed three types of provision for pupils with additional needs:

- **A Communication Centre**, which is for pupils who have speech, language and social communication needs, including autism, and specific language impairment (SLI). Some places are funded by the LA so that pupils from other schools in the borough can attend. Other pupils may come to the school for one or two sessions a week
- **A Support Centre** where pupils with a variety of social and emotional health needs can be given specialist help to overcome problems relating to attendance, attitudes to attainment, bereavement, self-esteem, sustaining relationships, etc. Relevant specialists consider the entirety of a student's needs and then individual or group support is given for a limited period. After this time, students may move on to receive longer term support, for instance, from a counsellor or learning mentor.
- **A Learning Centre** where pupils with a variety of learning needs can be given individual or targeted small group work. Some will have conditions such as: specific learning difficulties (SpLD) including dyslexia, AD(H)D, Down's syndrome, fragile x, or general learning difficulties. Their progress is audited on a termly basis and provision mapping is used. There are alternative pathways for them at key stage 4, including Entry Level Certificates.

To enable the three centres to work effectively, the school has gathered together a team of specialist teachers, speech and language therapists, educational psychologists and high level teaching assistants (HLTAs), in addition to counsellors and learning mentors.

The school formed a working group to consider how to present the *SEN Information Report*, which is also the basis of its contribution to the LA's *Local Offer*. The result appeared on the school's website in September 2014. As well as describing the three Centres, parents and pupils can be heard giving their views on the difference the support they receive has made to their progress. This is a very direct example of how families can be involved in developing the schools' SEN Information Report and bring it to life. (The SEN Information Report that all schools need to have on their websites and update annually was mentioned in the previous chapter.)

David Bartram says he is in favour of the change of terminology in the SEND Code from behaviour, emotional and social development (BESD) to social, emotional and mental health difficulties (SEMH). He sees it both as a step forward in not over-identifying students as having SEN, when their behaviour has some other cause, and also in terms of the focus it gives to looking at students' social and emotional needs, rather than trying to keep their behaviour under control. He sees an inclusive school as one in which an emphasis on valuing individual differences leads all pupils, irrespective of social or cultural background, disability or difficulty in learning, to succeed in terms of the fulfilment of academic and social goals, as well as the development of positive attitudes towards themselves and towards others. He says: 'The support pupils need may be academic, or social, cultural or emotional. We have put in place a number of systems to help this inclusive view of education'. There is more about Lampton's role as a teaching school in Chapter 9 of this book.

Special schools and inclusion

There was a time when inclusion was seen solely in terms of the inclusion of pupils with SEND in mainstream settings. With the growth of a continuum of SEND provision, there is a better understanding that all schools, whether mainstream, with or without units, or special, may or may not be inclusive of all the people in their school community. Also, that there are different ways of being inclusive, as these case studies have shown. For the majority of children and young people with SEND, this will mean being supported in a mainstream class. For others, it will be having more specialist input within a mainstream setting, while for those with the most complex needs, it may mean being in an environment that will enable them to access the curriculum in different ways and at a different level and pace.

A case study of special school provision

The final case study in this chapter is of Whitefield Schools and Centre. The current executive principal, Elaine Colquhoun, a former president of the National Association for SEN (Nasen), was appointed in 2011. On 1 April 2014, Whitefield Schools and its partner school, Joseph Clarke School, an all-age school for pupils with a visual impairment (VI), became a Multi-Academy Trust (MAT) known as the Whitefield Academy Trust. As the school had previously been a grant maintained school and then a foundation school, Elaine explained that a move to academy status seemed the next logical step. (The various types of academies, including MATs, are described in the next chapter. Chapter 9 describes Whitefield's work as a teaching school.)

Case study

Whitefield Schools and Centre, Waltham Forest

Whitefield Schools and Centre is a special school complex in Walthamstow. It has 340 pupils on the main site and a further 100 at the VI school.

Forty-nine different nationalities are represented. The various elements of the complex are as follows:

- The Margaret Brearley School (all-age, for complex needs)
- The Peter Turner Primary School
- The Niels Chapman Secondary School

[These three are named after previous head teachers of Whitefield]

- A classroom at Waltham Forest College
- A Research and Development Centre
- The LA's Support Services for HI, VI, autism and learning difficulties.

The Joseph Clarke School for VI pupils aged 2–19, which is part of the MAT, is on a different site.

Whitefield accepts pupils with a very wide range of needs. Most of them have severe learning difficulties (SLD), or profound and multiple learning difficulties (PMLD), well over half have a diagnosis of autism, over 10% are deafblind (also referred to as multi-sensory impairment), and about 5% have a diagnosis of specific language impairment (SLI). With such a wide spread of needs across pre-school to post-16, Elaine describes the curriculum as 'bespoke', with the aim being for every pupil to follow a curriculum that matches their interests and level of ability.

The school used to offer GCSEs and, occasionally, even A levels, through linking with other establishments, but with the changes to the examination system, combined with the increase in complexity of the pupil population, this is no longer the case. However, the link with Waltham Forest College means that there are vocational routes for pupils who reach 16. In addition, the school is one of the special schools in this country using Project Search, which started in the USA as a direct employment route for students with SEND (see Chapter 6).

As another example of the changing population, Elaine mentioned that there are 50 pupils who have to be tube fed, rather than just a handful. There are several nurses on site, a physiotherapist, a music therapist and the school buys in additional speech and language therapy hours and educational psychology as needed.

Very much in keeping with the main principles of the SEND Code of Practice, the school has a family support team and a programme of events, so that families from all backgrounds feel included in their children's education. In 2013, the team won the Leading Parent Partnership Award (LPPA), a national award which recognises schools at the forefront of effective parental engagement (see Chapter 8).

This chapter has tried to show how schools of all kinds are responding to having a more complex population of pupils. This has brought more challenges to all teachers in terms of the need to adapt the environment and the curriculum. It shows that for all teachers to see themselves as teachers of pupils with SEND, means that they need to be not only more flexible in their approach, but also better informed about special needs.

Further reading

For additional information, you can refer to the relevant sections of the SEND Code of Practice 2015:
SEND Code of Practice 2015: Chapter 4 – The Local Offer.

DCSF (2007) *Planning and Developing Special Educational Provision: A Guide for Local Authorities and other Proposers.* Nottingham: DCSF.

DfE (2014d) *Supporting Pupils at School with Medical Conditions.* Department for Education.

DfE (2014e) *Templates: Supporting Pupils with Medical Conditions.* Department for Education.

Dittrich, W. and Tutt, R (2008) *Educating Children with Complex Conditions: Understanding Overlapping and Co-existing Disorders.* London: Sage.

5

Local authorities working with schools to increase SEN provision

Chapter overview

This chapter looks at the pressures of a growing pupil population and its impact on meeting the needs of children and young people with SEND. The effect on local authorities of the 'academisation' of schools is considered, as well as the growth of free schools. There is an example of how one LA is working with its schools to develop the extra provision that is needed.

This is followed by a case study of a SEND Pathfinder authority. As well as a reference to the LA's work with free schools, which is one way of widening choice for children, young people and their families, the chapter provides an insight into how the Pathfinders have helped to set in train the change in culture that the 2015 SEND Code of Practice requires.

The chapter ends with examples of free schools that are being established for learners with autism across the 0–25 age range.

Changes to the pupil population

At the time the reforms to the SEND system were being implemented, it was known that there would continue to be a rise in the number of children starting primary education. The *Statistical First Release: National Pupil Projections – Future Trends in Pupil Numbers* (DfE, 2014i) estimated that by 2023, pupil numbers would be 9% higher than in 2014, a time when they were already on the increase. From this, it was projected that secondary schools would experience the upturn in numbers from 2016. This presented a major challenge to local authorities (LAs), as their ability to build new schools has been limited since the Academies Act of 2010. Although they continue to be responsible for providing enough places for pupils, any new schools are supposed to be academies, including the type of academy known as a free school.

Academisation

Academies were first established under Labour, but when the Coalition Government came to power in May 2010, they were keen to accelerate the programme and also to introduce free schools, which can be set up by groups of people with an interest in education. Academies are described, rather confusingly, as publicly funded independent schools, as they are not managed by a local authority. Other differences are that they do not have to follow the national curriculum; they can set the pay and conditions of their staff; and alter the length of school terms. However, they do have to follow the same laws on admissions, SEN and exclusions, as well as sharing their facilities with other schools and with the community.

Key point: Academies

Academies are run by academy trusts, which are charitable companies limited by guarantee. As well as converter academies (schools that have chosen to convert to academy status) and sponsored academies (which often replace schools that are considered to be doing less well), academies may be:

- Stand-alone academies
- Multi-Academy Trusts (MATs) – an example of a MAT is Whitefield (see previous chapter)
- Umbrella Trusts, where, unlike MATs, schools share governance arrangements but have separate trusts.

Types of academies include:

- Free schools
- University Technical Colleges (UTCs) for 14–19-year-olds
- Studio Schools, also for 14–19-year-olds.

The type of academy that has impacted most on increasing provision for pupils with SEN, has been the free schools. There is further information on this development, both in this chapter and in Chapter 8.

The academies programme in relation to provision for children and young people who have SEND is important on two counts. Firstly, it alters the relationship between schools and their local authority. As LAs have a continuing responsibility for all pupils with SEND regardless of what type of school they attend, this is important. Secondly, academies, particularly in the shape of free schools, are increasing the range of provision available to some pupils with SEND.

Building new schools

Although the DfE, in *School Organisation (Maintained Schools)* (2014j) gave a little more flexibility to LAs as regards trying to achieve the additional places needed in most areas, it remained a requirement that they had to endeavour to find a sponsor to establish an academy or free school in order to build a new school. The organisation that looks after the creation of free schools is called the New Schools Network (NSN). There is more about free schools later in this chapter and in Chapter 8, which considers specialist and alternative provision.

Changes to the SEN pupil population

As well as the growth in the general pupil population, the information on SEND pupils and where they are being educated, originates from the Special Educational Needs (Information) Act 2008, which came into force in 2009. Since then, governments have had to report annually on what is happening to pupils with special needs. The *Statistical First Release: Special Educational Needs in England* (DfE, 2014k), published in September 2014, shows that the oft quoted figure of one in five pupils having SEN has remained fairly constant, although it rose above this prior to 2009 and then dipped below from 2012 onwards (see Table 5.1).

Table 5.1   Some SEN statistics

	2007	2008	2009	2010	2011	2012	2013	2014
SEN pupils								
% non-statemented	16.5	17.3	17.9	18.3	17.8	17.0	16.0	15.1
% with statements	2.8	2.8	2.8	2.8	2.8	2.8	2.8	2.8
% of all SEN	19.3	20.1	20.7	21.1	20.6	19.8	18.8	17.9
% of statemented pupils in mainstream schools	57.2	56.2	55.2	54.6	54.2	53.6	52.9	51.9
% of statemented pupils in special schools*	37.9	38.8	39.4	40.2	40.6	40.9	41.4	42.2

Note: *Includes maintained special schools (35.9%–40.5%) and non-maintained special schools (2.0%–1.7%). It does not include the small number of pupils with SEN who are in pupil referral units (PRUs) or independent schools.

Source: DfE (2014k), national tables: SFR 26/2014.

From 2009 to 2014, while the number of pupils with SEN but without statements declined, those with statements remained the same. This might be expected to continue at around 2.8%, as the government has sought to reassure parents that replacing statements with Education, Health and Care Plans (EHC Plans) is not a cost-cutting exercise, and it expects the criteria for getting an EHC Plan to remain the same as for a statement. (The whole of chapter 9 in the 2014 SEND Code of Practice explains the change from statements to EHC Plans, both in terms of new EHC Plans and in terms of how to make the transition from statements to EHC Plans.)

Research undertaken by Leslie and Skidmore and written up in their publication, *SEN: The Truth about Inclusion* (2007), indicated that between 1997 and 2007, nearly 9,000 special school places were lost. Since their study, with the rise in pupil numbers generally and the increasing complexity of children's needs, many special schools throughout England have found themselves being asked to admit additional pupils, and the numbers in maintained special schools in January 2014 had increased to 96,545, which means that the numbers identified as being lost in Leslie and Skidmore's research are well on the way to being restored.

A case study of a London borough

To illustrate this growth in demand for special school places, the first case study is of the London Borough of Brent and two of its special schools. Out of the borough's school population,19.1% of pupils have special needs, 2.7% have statements and 0.9% attend special schools. The LA has a wide spread of provision for pupils with SEND, including additionally resourced provision in mainstream schools for pupils with autism, hearing impairment (HI), moderate learning difficulties (MLD) and speech, language and communication needs (SLCN). It has a number of support services, two PRUs, one free school and five special schools. In 2013, the council's forecast was that 91 additional places would be needed in special schools by 2020. This was for 32 pupils with autism and a further 59 who have severe learning difficulties (SLD). In the public consultation, the council wrote that the extra places would 'Provide parents with increased options for special school places'. As has been mentioned before, giving parents a greater degree of choice is one of the main principles of the SEND Code of Practice. A project group of representatives from education, health, schools and social services was set up by the LA, to support the implementation of these changes.

The case study that follows is of two special schools that worked with the LA to bring about a solution to this rise in demand. Both schools have a high percentage of pupils from a wide range of ethnic minority groups, as well as a much higher than average number of pupils on free school meals, who attract extra funding through the pupil premium.

Key point: Pupil premium

The pupil premium was introduced in April 2011 as a way of helping to raise the attainment of disadvantaged pupils. The amount has risen year by year and in 2014/15 was as follows:

- £1,300 for primary-aged pupils eligible for free school meals (FSM)
- £935 for secondary-aged pupils eligible for FSM
- £1,900 for looked after pupils or those adopted from care
- £300 for children of service personnel.

Pupil Premium Awards have been introduced and will continue to be awarded to 500 primary, secondary or special schools in 2015 and 2016. The Bridge Academy, which is mentioned in Chapter 8 of this book, was a national runner-up in 2014.

Woodfield School has had additional building work in order to accommodate its growing population. The head teacher, Desi Lodge Patch, has worked closely with the LA on a shared vision for meeting the increasingly complex needs of pupils. The Village School, which was formed by amalgamating two special schools, moved into a completely new building in September 2013, again as a result of agreeing with the LA the provision that was going to become necessary.

Case study

Woodfield School and The Village School, Brent

Woodfield is a special school for 11–19-year-olds who have moderate or severe learning difficulties and may also have autism. Over three years, there has been a 38.8% increase in pupils on the autism spectrum. Woodfield has had specialist school status for sports and ICT since 2009 and was designated as a teaching school in 2013, with a specific focus on pupils with special needs. From September 2014, the numbers went up from 136 to 176. When pupils reach Year 9, some start a gradual transfer to a local high school, where there is an Inclusion Centre, so that they are ready to transfer full-time for Year 10. This enables those who have the skills to benefit from a mainstream curriculum to complete their education with their mainstream peers, while continuing to benefit from an enhanced level of support in order to do so.

(Continued)

(Continued)

Woodfield takes a holistic view of its pupils. As well as a sensory room, it has a room for Drawing and Talking Therapy. The school employs a drama therapist, a speech and language therapist and trained language assistants, a counsellor and a family worker from TaMHS (Targeted Mental Health in Schools).

The Village School has 235 pupils aged 2–19 and caters for a very wide range of needs, including all levels of learning difficulty, communication problems and autism, as well as for those who have physical, medical and sensory impairments. The staff of 185 includes therapists, family workers and personal care staff. All staff undertake an extensive and comprehensive training programme, and the school has been awarded the Gold CPLD Quality Mark (Continuing Professional Learning and Development). The Village School has been built with the needs of its complex population at its heart. Its facilities include: sensory rooms to meet the needs of HI, VI and deafblind children, recreational areas for PMLD pupils, a sensory garden, a hydrotherapy pool, a roof play area, extensive facilities for speech, music and drama therapy, and a community shop and café manned by pupils.

The head teacher, Kay Charles, says the school takes pride in its inclusive philosophy and its partnerships with local schools, including Kingsbury High School, to support pupils taking accredited courses at KS4 and KS5 on a part-time basis. The link with the London Borough of Brent has been very important in delivering a commitment that all children can make progress and that it is their entitlement to do.

In developing Brent's local offer, John Galligan, School Improvement Team Manager at Brent Council, explained that a steering group was established consisting of the Brent Schools Partnership, Health and LA officers, with multi-agency subgroups established for the age groups 0–5, 5–11, 11–16 and 16–25 and with the involvement of parents, carers and young people. In their contribution to the LA's Local Offer, the head teacher of Woodfield says they have stressed that 'We have a school ethos with inclusion at its heart and believe that all pupils on their personalised pathway will make outstanding progress. We will work with parents to make sure they feel valued and listened to, with up-to-date information readily available'. Like Lampton School in the previous chapter, Woodfield is a Senior Partner and a hub leader in the Challenge Partnership. (This is explained further in Chapter 9 of this book.)

Although John Galligan said that the delay in publishing the SEND Code of Practice had resulted in a tight timescale for implementation, he felt that the reforms had helped colleagues and stakeholders to focus on the quality of provision in both schools and support services, as well as improving engagement with parents. This comment fits in with the findings of some of the SEND Pathfinder LAs, who reported that families found the person-centred approach to Education, Health and Care needs assessments and Plans, involved them far more than when they had undergone the statementing process. This was the case whether or not their child or young person received an EHC Plan after being assessed. Some LAs, such as Darlington, which was another Pathfinder authority, decided to use a One Plan. This meant that all the information collected as part of the assessment was not wasted, but put together in one plan that was used to identify what the young person and the family would like to achieve and the support that would be put in place to meet their aspirations. As with EHC Plans and statements, the One Plan is regularly monitored and reviewed.

An example of an SEND Pathfinder authority

As explained in the second chapter of this book, SEND Pathfinders were established to pilot some of the new ways of working and to prepare non-Pathfinder areas to implement the changes to the SEN Framework from September 2014. The next case study is of an LA which was part of the Pathfinder programme throughout its various stages. It illustrates the work of the Pathfinders in practical terms and the partnership working involved, in order to effect the change in culture required by the SEND Code of Practice 2014.

Hertfordshire local authority (LA)

Hertfordshire was one of the original 20 Pathfinders set up in 2011 and later became a Pathfinder champion for the Eastern region, supporting other LAs in preparing for the changes. In the final phase of the programme, from April 2014 to March 2015, the LA worked with Bedford Borough and the delivery partners Early Support, Preparing for Adulthood, Contact a Family and the National Network of Parent Carer Forums (NNPCF), to form a regional team offering co-ordinated support to the LAs in the Eastern Region. Herts also took on a national role, and, with Manchester, led on the theme of Preparing for Adulthood (see chapter 8 of the SEND Code of Practice). Debbie Orton, Head of Integrated Services for Learning (ISL), in the LA's Children's Services, explained that there were a number of factors that put Hertfordshire in a strong position to work with its schools. Firstly, in the wake of a number of schools becoming academies, the LA, together with its schools, whether academies or not, established Herts for Learning (HfL), with the idea of encouraging greater autonomy through a new model for providing local school improvement and business support services. After the four years it took to become fully established, in 2012, HfL was up and running as a not-for-profit company, providing a wide range of services. The company is led by schools, with 96% of all schools (486 in total) owning shares in the company. Six school leaders are elected as directors, while the LA has two nominated directors and a 20% shareholding.

Another way in which the LA and its schools were used to working together was one that was specific to SEN. The 'Developing Special Provision Locally' (DSPL) approach established nine area groups across the county, each one involving school leaders, parents from the local community and LA officers. Funding is devolved to each area for children and young people with high-level SEN and, with it, the responsibility for commissioning services and provision for that community. Each area is led by a mainstream school head teacher, and Debbie said that moving the balance of accountability from the centre to groups of schools in this way, fits in well with the close working with parents and with schools that the Pathfinder work, especially the development of the Local Offer, required.

Case study

Hertfordshire SEND Pathfinder

Hertfordshire is a large county which is often seen as quite affluent. However, it has pockets of high deprivation as well. Out of the school population, 16% of pupils are identified as having SEN, with 1.4% having statements and 0.7% being placed in special schools. There are 25 special schools, a wide range of units and bases attached to mainstream schools, a range of centrally funded services and seven PRUs (known locally as ESCs – education support centres), plus one LA-maintained Alternative Provision (AP). Of the 81 academies, 52 are secondary mainstream schools, two are special schools and one of the ESCs is now an AP academy. There are four FE colleges and all contributed to the Pathfinder work. From the time of free schools first coming onto the scene, the LA has worked closely with groups wishing to set up free schools, and the West Herts Community Trust, which runs three free schools, has the LA, the University of Hertfordshire and head teachers on its Board.

Debbie Orton said that the work was made easier by only having two Clinical Commissioning Groups (CCGs) to work with and that, together, their boundaries were coterminous with Herts. This led to an agreement that, for instance, there would be a Lead for speech and language therapy to manage work across the LA.

When it came to helping schools with their contribution to the LA's local offer, a format was provided for mainstream schools, while the special schools needed to take a more individual approach. Both were based on the 13 points needed to complete the SEN Information Report, with each school expected to say how each of the issues were being addressed. The same format, with some adjustments, was used for early years providers and for colleges. The DSPL approach of involving local collectives of parents and schools and other settings to work strategically together to shape the services, fits well with the Local Offer. The work with parents was mainly carried out through parents on the DSPL areas, Herts Parent Carer Involvement (HPCI), which is part of the NNPCF, and the Parent

Partnership Service (PPS), now renamed the Information, Advice and Support Service (IASS), who were involved in training the Independent Supporters funded by the government to help parents find their way through the new SEN system. Debbie explained that one of their findings was the different approaches needed to work with parents who were already in the system and those who were coming into it as the reforms were taking place.

As well as holding sessions for schools, parents and other partners to become familiar with the changes, there was a major drive to help LA staff switch to having a much more hands-on role. For instance, those who had been used to being SEN officers without necessarily having much direct contact with the families involved, needed to become used to having face-to-face communication with families. Many of them found the change to co-ordinating the work involved in an EHC needs assessment and Plan and, in some cases, becoming the family's key worker, made them appreciate the benefits to families, who felt they were being listened to. Debbie stressed that discussions around the development of the Local Offer and EHC Plans had been very positive in identifying parents' strategic role in the changes and in improving the system. Next, it was a question of making sure everyone felt part of the process including bringing services together across the 0–25 age range. However, through the Pathfinder work, the foundations for integrated working had been laid.

Talking about the team's involvement as a SEND Pathfinder, Debbie and her colleagues said that, although linking up different services and people had been very time consuming at the start, and there had to be a huge commitment in terms of resources, there was no doubt that the experience had been beneficial on many levels. The services had gained a much better understanding of each other's work; staff had seen the benefits of working more closely with families; and the families themselves had valued being involved in decision making, both at an individual and a strategic level.

Activity

In the case study of a Pathfinder LA, the following delivery partners (who are voluntary and community sector organisations), were mentioned:

- Early Support
- Preparing for Adulthood
- Contact a Family
- NNPCF.

(Continued)

(Continued)

Explore each of their websites and look for any resources or information that are relevant to your situation.

www.councilfordisabledchildren.org.uk/earlysupport
www.preparingforadulthood.org.uk
www.cafamily.org.uk
www.nnpcf.org.uk

Provision for pupils with autism

A major difficulty for many LAs has been to provide sufficient places for the rising numbers of pupils being diagnosed with autism. Over a comparatively short time, autism has moved from being described as a low incidence need to one of the five most common (see Chapter 9 of this book for information about the most common conditions). Since the 1990s, it has seemed that as fast as LAs have tried to increase their provision, the more numerous the autism population has become. The reasons for this are beyond the scope of this book to explore, but part of the explanation may be that there is better diagnosis and that autism is now seen as a spectrum that includes Asperger's syndrome.

The first part of this chapter looked at the pressures on schools due to a rising pupil population, as well as an increase in the complexity of children's needs. It also considered the need for LAs to work with organisations or groups of people wishing to set up free schools, as a way of increasing the number of school places available. Some of the free schools that have been established have been special schools, including schools for pupils on the autism spectrum. The final case study in this chapter draws on the developments in this field by the National Autistic Society (NAS), a long-standing charity founded by parents, and Ambitious About Autism (AAA), which is another national charity set up to support children and young people up to the age of 25.

Case study

Free schools for pupils with autism

NAS schools   The National Autistic Society has nearly 50 years' experience of running schools. More recently, the charity has formed the NAS Academies Trust (NASAT) which is sponsoring a number of academies and free schools, NAS schools are based on the belief that children and young people with autism have the right to an appropriate education that meets their very individual needs. Their first free school, Thames

Valley School for 5–16 year olds, opened in Reading in 2013 and has 50 places for day pupils. Two more schools are due to open in 2015. Church Lawton School in Stoke-on-Trent will be for 5–19 year olds and The Vanguard School in Lambeth will be for 11–19 year olds.

The plan is to be part of a continuum of provision for pupils with autism, including outreach work to local schools and facilitating moves back to mainstream or part-time provision. A number of LAs have been working closely with the NAS to provide more places for pupils who need autism-specific education, recognising its links to the wider autism community and its focus on supporting students to achieve positive outcomes after they leave.

Autism Schools Trust   The Autism Schools Trust (AST) aims to create schools that use evidence-based approaches to enable children with autism to learn and succeed. The Trust is sponsored by two organisations, Ambitious about Autism and Dimensions – both not-for-profit organisations with a wealth of experience in supporting children and adults with autism. The AST was formed in December 2012 to support the setting up of its first school, The Rise School.

The Rise School supports children and young people with autism aged 4–19 to access a broad and challenging curriculum alongside mainstream pupils. Based in West London, it is located on the site of a mainstream school (Feltham Community College), enabling pupils to access a wide range of learning and social opportunities, whilst still receiving the specialist help they need. The school supports its pupils in accessing further learning and work beyond school and making a successful transition to adult life. The AST is in talks with a number of LAs with a view to opening more autism-specific schools from September 2016.

This final case study leads into the next chapter, which examines further the increase in the age range up to 25 years. It is also concerned with bringing together the work of the different services, which the SEND Pathfinders have helped to encourage.

Further reading

For additional information, you can refer to the relevant sections of the SEND Code of Practice 2015:
SEND Code of Practice (2015): Chapter 9 – Education, Health and Care needs assessments and Plans.

DfE/DoH (2014b) *Transition to the New 0 to 25 Special Educational Needs and Disability System: Statutory Guidance for Local Authorities and Organisations Providing Services to Children and Young People with SEN*, www.gov.uk/government/publications
DfE/DoH (2014c) *Implementing a New 0 to 25 Special Needs System: LAs and Partners. Duties and Timescales – What You Must Do When*, www.gov.uk/government/publications
Jordan, R. (2013) *Autism with Severe Learning Difficulties*, 2nd edn. London: Souvenir Press.
Leslie, C. and Skidmore, C. (2008) *SEN: The Truth about Inclusion*. London: The Bow Group.

Provision across the services and up to 25 years

Chapter overview

This chapter focuses on two significant changes in the way the SEND system operates in the wake of the Children and Families Act and the SEND Code of Practice 2015. These are:

- A change in culture that sees education, health and social care working much more closely together, in order to take a more holistic view of the needs of children, young people and their families
- The change to the age range that SEN covers, now 0–25 years.

Case studies include, Project Search, which helps young people into employment; a mainstream secondary school working with other services to provide a safe and secure environment; a special secondary school that has developed 19–25 provision; and a charity working closely with the NHS to provide for children and young adults.

Bringing the services together

This is the final chapter in Part Two of this book, which has been looking at provision. There have been many attempts to have closer working between those who work in education, health and social care. This is particularly important in the case of children and young people with SEND as they may need the support of health and/or social care as well as education.

One of the main principles outlined in chapter 1 of the SEND Code of Practice is about the collaboration of the three services in providing the support that is needed:

> If children and young people with SEN or disabilities are to achieve their ambitions and the best possible educational and other outcomes, including getting a job and living as independently as possible, local education, health and social care services should work together to ensure they get the right support. (paragraph 1.22)

Indeed, the whole of chapter 3 of the Code is headed: 'Working together across education, health and care for joint outcomes'. It includes information on:

- Establishing effective partnerships with children, young people and their families, as well as across education, health and social care
- Joint planning, commissioning and delivery, including regional commissioning to meet low incidence needs (such as profoundly deaf children or those who are registered blind)
- Roles and responsibilities, including a new role for a Designated Medical Officer (DMO) or Designated Clinical Officer (DCO).

A previous attempt to bring this about was the Children Act of 2004, which was based on the Green Paper, *Every Child Matters*. Since then, Local Education Authorities (LEAs) have disappeared and been replaced by Local Authorities (LAs). As a general pattern, these incorporate education and social care under a Director of Children's Services. So, since then, there has been closer working between education and social care, whereas health has often remained the odd one out.

The health service

Meanwhile, the health service has undergone several transformations of its own. When the SEND Green Paper came out, in March 2011, the link was seen as being with Primary Care Trusts (PCTs), which were established in April 2002. However, in April 2013, they were replaced by Clinical Commissioning Groups (CCGs). As well as restructuring, another difficulty in the engagement of health has been the fact that, unlike education and social care, the boundaries may not be coterminous. Because of these difficulties and the problems in the past with getting health involved, there has been a determination throughout the process of making changes to the SEN Framework, to tie in health and to involve health professionals in the changes. For instance, much of the documentation that has been issued has come from the Department for Education (DfE) and the Department of Health (DoH), while some of the correspondence, including the Foreword to the SEND Code of Practice, has been signed by Dr Dan Poulter, Parliamentary Under-Secretary of State for Health and Edward Timpson, Parliamentary Under-Secretary of State for Children and Families (the role of the latter includes responsibility for children and young people with special needs).

An initiative involving the health service

It would be wrong, however, to imply that all the pressure to be involved is coming from legislation. As an example of health professionals' willingness to find ways of extending opportunities for young people with SEND, there is a number of hospitals in England that have become involved in 'Project SEARCH', which started in the USA as a way of helping young people with significant disabilities to make the transition from school into the world of work.

Key point: Project SEARCH 🔑

Project SEARCH is a one-year school-to-work programme based entirely in the workplace, with the aim of achieving employment at the end of it. Throughout a year's programme, students work on improving their basic skills, as well as the additional skills they need to work successfully as an employee who is part of a team.

Although other organisations have also been involved in this country, hospitals have been the main supporters of this scheme, often working with special schools to provide a classroom within the hospital and offering students the opportunity to try their hand at working in different departments.

This has led to some young people with SEND getting into work rather than spending a lifetime being unemployed. Even for those who have not been successful in being offered, or holding down, a job, the skills they have learned have helped them to take up voluntary work or to be more involved in their communities in other ways.

The British Association for Supported Employment (base) has reported that between 2012 and 2014 the number of Project Search sites in the UK rose from 17 to 32. An evaluation of the Project carried out in 2013 and published in 2014 (*Final Report: Evaluation of Employment Outcomes of Project Search UK*) by Axel Kaehne showed that most of the students started the programme between 16 and 25, with a peak at 19 years. The programme showed an average employment rate of over 50%. Whitefield Schools and Centre, which was featured as a case study in Chapter 4 of this book, has been part of Project Search.

Case study

An example of Project Search

This example explains the work of Whitefield Schools and Centre with Whipps Cross Hospital. Although some pupils had previously been well placed in local or specialist colleges and others in social care provision, very few were able to move into employment, even when they were capable of doing so. Project Search has been able to help fill this gap.

The programme began with a small group of students in 2013 and has grown since then. The hospital has provided a classroom for the students, where they can continue to improve their basic skills with a teacher from the school and also have the support of two Job Coaches. In addition, they join the staff of the hospital as trainees, working in different departments to learn new skills and to be in a stronger position to apply for posts when they are advertised.

The head teacher, Elaine Colquhoun, says the fresh opportunities have seen them grow in confidence, as they have risen to the challenge of meeting the public, carrying out audits and learning some technical skills. Their teacher, Jamie Bargeman, adds that each batch of students has hit the ground running. They have followed an induction programme, which has included learning about fire safety procedures and infection control, as well as the behaviour expected of employees. After this, they have had internships in five of the hospital's departments: orthodontics, portering, pharmacy, medical library and out patients/new appointments. Seeing the maturity with which they have risen to the challenge, Jamie says, has made other departments keen to come on board for future rotation placements. In September 2014, all students were in permanent, full-time posts, either at the hospital or elsewhere.

In its second year of running the programme, Whitefield is working with the local council to provide an option for placements in a different setting. Beyond this, a senior member of staff is exploring how to develop 19–25 provision in partnership with both health and social care, to help address the needs of the extended age range identified in the SEND Code of Practice. Sources of funding are being sought to enable this to happen.

Social care

There are many occupations where professionals are more likely to be noticed when something goes wrong than for all the work they carry out successfully. A useful strategy for encouraging pupils to behave is said to be to catch children doing the right thing rather than drawing attention to their misdemeanours. Yet, the same strategy is seldom applied to adults. Social workers have a particularly difficult role, whereby their work so often goes unrecognised, but, as soon as a mistake is made, they are in danger of being pilloried in the Press. In 2013, the Department for Education (DfE) launched an Innovation Programme to encourage different ways of supporting vulnerable children.

Key point: Children's Care Innovation Programme 🔑

The programme hopes to achieve change, so that, in a few years' time: children receiving support from the social care system have better life chances; there are stronger incentives for innovation and replication of successful new approaches; and there is better value for money.

The programme covers two key areas:

1. Improving the quality and impact of children's social work
2. Rethinking the support for adolescents who are in, or on the edge of, care.

The delivery partner with the DfE for this programme is the Spring Consortium (www.springconsortium.com).

Speaking at the Children's Social Care Innovation Summit in July 2014, Edward Timpson gave a speech confirming that £30 million had been set aside for 2014 and more in succeeding years, if enough bids that are transformative in their approach are put forward. He talked of the need to do things differently in order to improve services, pointing out that LAs had the freedom to outsource social care elements. A few LAs have started to do this, or to work together as a group of LAs to strengthen the service they offer.

The Tri-borough LAs of Hammersmith & Fulham, Kensington & Chelsea and Westminster, for example, made a successful bid to redesign their entire children's social care system from within, in a way that gave professionals more time with children and families, and with practice being rooted in greater expertise and evidence. Extra time was created for working with families, by cutting back on bureaucracy and changing the focus from plans and paperwork to effective, hands on, intensive work. Families with the most complex needs have been given one key person to work with them. The idea of a key worker was also found to be something families appreciated who trialled the transition from statements to Education, Health and Care Plans (EHC Plans). The Tri-borough way of working is mentioned again in Chapter 8 of this book, with reference to the way in which the LAs came together to provide a better system of Alternative Provision.

Questions for reflection

In a school or educational setting that you know: what are the links with health professionals?

1. Are there ways in which their involvement could be increased or improved?
2. What are the links with social care?
3. What else might be done to provide a more joined up approach to working with children and young people with SEND and their families?
4. If you know examples of effective partnerships with health and/or social care, how have you, or might you, spread the word?

Case study of a girls' secondary school

The next case study in this chapter is of a girls' secondary school in London which has a focus on involving its pupils and its parents at the strategic level and being actively involved with the local community. As an example of its community work, which involves working closely with other services, the school has worked with the Local Safeguarding Children's Board (LSCB) to share how it has found innovative ways of engaging pupils and their families in keeping children and young people safe within a diverse community. As well as giving presentations, the school has written up its effective practice so that it can be used by other schools and agencies.

Key point: Local Safeguarding Children's Boards (LSCBs)

LSCBs were established in every locality by the Children Act of 2004, as a way of bringing together all those organisations and services concerned with the safeguarding and welfare of children.

In the *Munro Review of Child Protection* (DfE, 2011c), Professor Munro said that LSCBs are crucial to improving multi-agency working in this area. Key organisations involved include:

- LAs and district councils
- The police and probation service
- NHS bodies
- Youth Offending Teams and Young Offender Institutions.

The head teacher of Bentley Wood High School, Janice Howkins, believes that high aspirations need to be underpinned by a safe and secure environment where students are happy and keen to learn.

Case study

Bentley Wood High School, Harrow

Bentley Wood is a secondary academy of over 1,000 girls aged 11–18, two-thirds of whom are from ethnic minority families. The school converted to academy status in 2011. It specialises in mathematics, computing and science. There are 50 feeder primary schools and there is a high mobility rate amongst the pupils. The school is part of the Harrow Collegiate, so that its sixth form students can study at a number of other schools and colleges, while remaining part of the school.

Janice Howkins describes the school as a comprehensive and inclusive school. For example, the SEND Policy has been changed to an Inclusion and Innovation Policy. Assessment, support and the tracking of progress are carried out by an Inclusion and Innovation team. However, all staff are expected to work in partnership with other relevant agencies, including LA Support Services, Health and Social Services and with relevant local and national voluntary organisations as well.

Older students who volunteer are trained by Childline to be Peer Mentors, so that they can be empathetic listeners, ready to talk through possible solutions to any concerns a student may have. In addition to the Student Council, pupils are involved with curriculum and school development as: Learning Leaders, Creative Leaders, Digital Leaders, STEM Leaders (Science, Technology, Engineering & Maths), Sports Leaders, Global Leaders and Media Leaders.

Parent Ambassadors are used to promote community cohesion by supporting families with induction and integration, encouraging parental involvement, addressing specific needs and raising awareness of the extended services available to families. There is also a Parent Voice Group which meets every half term with the head teacher and the assistant head teacher responsible for community cohesion so that they can be consulted on school development planning, strengthening still further the links between home and school.

The school's emphasis on expecting every teacher to take responsibility for all the students they teach, including those who have SEN or disabilities, is very much in harmony with the SEND Code of Practice. Likewise, the innovative ways that are used to involve students and their parents or carers in all aspects of the school's work and development, mirrors the Code's emphasis on children, young people and their families being at the heart of decisions that affect them and contributing to improving the SEN system as a whole.

Joined up working across the age range

The idea of stronger partnership working between the services is made even more necessary by the extension of SEND up to the age of 25 years. When Sarah Teather, who was the Minister responsible for SEN at the time the Green Paper, *Support and Aspiration: A New Approach to SEN and Disability* (DfE, 2011a), was published, spoke about her meetings with parents, two themes frequently emerged. The first was how upset they were at having to tell the story of their child's difficulties over and over again to different professionals, and the second was that their young people seemed to fall into a black hole when they left children's services, whether in social care or in health. The SEND Code of Practice, chapter 8: 'Preparing for Adulthood from the Earliest Years', includes a section on 'Transition to adult health services', and another on 'Transition to adult social care'.

In the first of these (paragraphs 8.54–8.56), it is explained that difficulties have sometimes arisen in the past as a young person moves from being under the care of a paediatrician to being looked after by different consultants and teams. To overcome this change, the Code says that:

> This means working with the young person to develop a transition plan, which identifies who will take the lead in co-ordinating care and referrals to other services. The young person should know who is taking the lead and how to contact them. (paragraph 8.54)

It goes on to explain that if the young person has an EHC Plan, the Plan itself will be the vehicle for co-ordinating the integration of health with other services. With reference to the transition to adult social care, paragraph 8.57 quotes the Care Act 2014, which went through Parliament at much the same time as the Children and Families Act. This states that:

> ... the local authority **must** carry out an adult care transition assessment where there is significant benefit to a young person or their carer in doing so and they are likely to have needs for care or support after turning 18. (paragraph 8.57)

There is further guidance if the young person has an EHC Plan, which explains how the two can be integrated.

Extending provision to 25 years

One of the changes that has received universal acclaim has been the extension of SEND to 25 years of age. As the majority of young people with special needs have cognitive difficulties, and their all-round development is likely to be delayed, to give them support for longer makes very good sense. Even those who are cognitively able will have other barriers to their learning, which may make it necessary for them to have continued support. There was some disappointment that, although Further Education (FE) is included in the Children and Families Act, Higher

Education (HE) has not been included. A minority of young people who have SEND, for instance those who have Asperger's syndrome, are severely dyslexic, or who have a significant sensory impairment, may be more than able to cope with the demands of a degree course, provided they have appropriate support. While many universities have done a considerable amount to welcome a wider group of students, the dropout rate from those who do not get enough support is unnecessarily high. Chapter 7 of the SEND Code of Practice is headed 'Further Education'. It covers what is expected by way of support for students, which mirrors to some extent the expectations on schools.

Provision for the older learner

It may be some time before there is sufficient provision and support for all those who need it up to the age of 25 years, but already there are examples of places that are moving in this direction. The next case study shows what can be achieved when schools, FE colleges, health and social care work together to create a provision that would be hard for any one organisation to provide on its own. The executive head teacher of St Andrew's school, Phil Harrison, says, 'We want our young people to be as well prepared for adult life as possible and we link up with a network of support with the vision that together we achieve more'. The school's aim is for all learners to 'start with the end in sight'. This ties in very closely with the SEND Code's emphasis throughout on the importance of specifying the outcomes children and families want and their aspirations for the future.

Case study 📁

St Andrew's School, Derby

St Andrew's is a school for learners aged 11–19 who have severe learning difficulties (SLD) and/or autism. It provides weekly residential provision as well as day places. It is a specialist school, a national support school and a teaching school with the Derby Teaching School Alliance (see Chapter 9 for more information).

It opened in 1978, and in 2010 Phil Harrison and Janine Cherrington, an FE specialist at the school, started exploring the possibility of creating a new specialist provision along the lines of a college for learners aged 19–25. Although these discussions preceded the changes to the SEN Framework of recognising young learners up to the age of 25, it was very much in line with the aim of having more local options for this age group, to allow young people to maintain essential community networks and continue to develop and implement skills acquired throughout their secondary education. The school has good links with Derby College, an FE College well known for its efforts to meet a wide range of needs. However, it did not suit all the school's diverse range of students and the only other option was specialist residential provision away from home.

To fill this gap, *Transition 2* was created to give school leavers the opportunity to develop the skills that would enable them to become more independent, to be part of the community, to gain experience of work and to learn the essential skills they would need to establish sustainable and meaningful opportunities in the future. In addition, it was designed to help them in developing the personal skills to keep themselves safe and healthy.

From November 2010 and over the next two years, the school worked with social care – both child and adult services – with health, the local council, local educational providers and the commissioners of provision in all these services, to complete the model. This led to the creation of a specialist team of staff, which includes educational, health and social care practitioners, with Janine Cherrington as Head of Service.

Transition 2 is on a separate site from the school and has its own newly modernised building, where each learner follows an individual pathway. The bespoke programmes can be full- or part-time. They can be formally accredited or RARPA (Recognising and Recording Progress and Achievement) based, and funded by the Employment and Support Allowance (ESA), which is drawn down through Derby College, or by using a Personal Budget. After years of planning, the new provision opened its doors in September 2012 having been developed as a partnership between St Andrew's School and Derby City Council. It gives young people the security of continuing their education locally, while helping them to consolidate and extend their skills and share their assets with the community. As well as the partners already mentioned, the support network includes: the Learning Disabilities Partnership Board; Local Area Coordination Derby; and the local Parent Carer Forum.

Integrated working across the age range

The final case study in this chapter is a clear demonstration of the overlapping nature of the two themes in the SEND Code of Practice of joint working and giving a greater range of opportunities to meet the needs of learners with SEND up to the age of 25.

Chailey Heritage Foundation is a registered charity which grew out of the Chailey Heritage School in Lewes, East Sussex. The school has a long history of providing specialist services for children and young people whose complex difficulties and significant medical needs require more than local services may be able to offer. Unusually, the school and NHS service operate from the same site, which covers several acres. Today, as well as the school, there are the services for young adults, which include a residential transition provision for 19–25-year-olds.

Helen Hewitt, the Chief Executive of Chailey Heritage Foundation, says that:

Inclusion is at the heart of our work. We are committed to giving each young person every opportunity to be as independent as they can, whether this is empowering them with independent mobility or communication skills to thrive in the 'mainstream' world, or enabling them to have a school and community life rather than isolation at home or in a hospital ward.

Case study 📁

Chailey Heritage Foundation

As well as the school for 3–19 year olds, which was established over 100 years ago, the Foundation has:

- Chailey Heritage Residential, offering flexible residential services for 3–19-year-olds
- Futures@Chailey Heritage, which is for young adults aged 19–25 (day and residential)
- Futures Life Skills Centre, which runs a wide range of daily activities for those adults who reside on site, as well as those living in the community
- Futures Hub, a day service for 19–25-year-olds.

The school itself caters for those who have complex physical needs and associated learning difficulties and is used by around 15 different LAs. Clinical and nursing care is provided by Chailey Heritage Clinical Services (part of Sussex Community NHS Trust), with placements being funded by the appropriate Clinical Commissioning Group (CCG). In recent years, there has been a marked increase in those who also have multi-sensory impairments (MSI). Around 80% of the pupils have a visual impairment (VI) and just under 20% have a dual sensory impairment. All pupils are wheelchair users, although a very few can walk short distances with assistance. Nearly all pupils are non-verbal and use a variety of communication techniques and aids.

All young people have access to high levels of clinical and therapeutic input, which is provided by the on-site NHS professionals. As well as a hydrotherapy pool, dark rooms with sensory trolleys are used for vision stimulation and assessment. The sensory rooms include a multi-sensory tunnel with switch-activated effects controlling many stimulating activities such as a bubble machine, a singing fish and a light tower. Horse riding is available and includes the possibility of working with a trained hippotherapist. All the teachers and classroom staff are highly skilled and have additional training to work with young people who have very complex needs.

Futures@ChaileyHeritage provides a stimulating environment where young adults are able to make choices and decisions about all areas of their lives, and plan for the future. This is achieved through person-centred planning, and working in partnership with young adults, their families and the organisation(s) that fund them. The individual packages of support may include accommodation, health and therapeutic services, life skills and a wide range of activities on site and in the community. Flexible packages of specialist residential care are available, ranging from short breaks to weekly, fortnightly, or 48 and 52 weeks. Teams of support workers provide 24-hour care backed by nursing staff from the Sussex Community NHS Trust.

The school's contribution to the Local Offer when it was first published in September 2014, was modelled on the pro forma used by the SE7 SEND Pathfinder (see Chapter 2 of this book for a description of the SE7 LAs and their work as one of the SEND Pathfinders throughout the programme). The school was part of the East Sussex Local Offer group and also contributed to the development of the Local Offer in two neighbouring LAs, representing non-maintained special schools.

Although the SEND Code of Practice addresses the needs of children and young people aged 0–25 regardless of whether they are at the milder or more severe end of the SEND continuum, the importance of services working together is thrown into sharp relief when the requirements of those with the most significant needs are considered. It is often said that the more complex a young person's needs are, the more the environment needs to be adjusted for them, rather than expecting them to fit in with what is provided for the majority. As the case studies in this chapter have made clear, this is not about removing them from their communities, but helping them to develop the confidence and the skills to take their place in society.

Further reading

For additional information, you can refer to the relevant sections of the SEND Code of Practice 2015:
SEND Code of Practice 2015: Chapter 8 – Preparing for adulthood from the earliest years.

DfE (2014) *Social Care: Guide to the 0–25 SEND Code of Practice*, www.gov.uk/government/publications

DfE/DoH (2014o) *0–25 SEND Code of Practice: A Guide for Health Professionals*, www.gov.uk/government/publications

Kaehne, A. (2014) *Final Report: Evaluation of Employment Outcomes of Project Search UK*: Liverpool: SWIE.

Kirby, A. (2013) *How to Succeed in College and University with Specific Learning Difficulties*. London: Souvenir Press.

PART THREE

PRACTICE

Meeting SEN in mainstream provision

> ### Chapter overview
>
> Chapter 7, which is the first of three chapters in Part 3 of this book looking at how practice is developing to meet new demands, focuses on mainstream provision across the age range. There is an explanation of the role of the SENCO (special educational needs co-ordinator) in different settings and case studies of: a nursery school and children's centre; a primary school with a very individual approach to meeting needs; and two secondary schools with contrasting, but equally effective, ways of being inclusive, one of which is part of an academy chain.
>
> Nurture groups are a feature of two of the case studies and there is reference to mental health issues in relation to children and young people who have SEND.

Mainstream provision

One of the key changes in the 2014 SEND Code of Practice is the move to ensuring that all teachers, whatever their role, see themselves as teachers of pupils who have special needs. This is particularly relevant in a mainstream context, as the vast majority of children and young people with SEND have always been educated in mainstream schools. Less than 3% of the school population has a statement or Education, Health and Care Plan (EHC Plan) and roughly half these pupils are in mainstream schools. So, mainstream teachers are responsible for educating all but about 1.5% of pupils who have the most complex needs. (The figures vary slightly depending on the local authority the child is in.) The most relevant chapters in the SEND Code of Practice in terms of the expectations on schools and other educational settings are:

- Chapter 5—Early Years Providers
- Chapter 6—Schools
- Chapter 7—Further Education.

The SEND Code's focus on every teacher seeing themselves as a teacher of pupils with SEND is explained in chapter 6 of the Code, where it states:

> Teachers are responsible and accountable for the progress and development of the pupils in their class, including where pupils access support from teaching assistants or specialist staff. (paragraph 6.36)

To a large extent, this has often been the expectation in primary schools, where pupils are likely to be with the same teacher for much of the day, but less so in secondary schools, where it is harder for subject teachers to understand the needs of a moving population of pupils who pass through their hands every week. Nevertheless, the Code makes it quite clear that, whether a teacher is responsible for a class or a subject, they are accountable for the progress of all their pupils and this will include any who have special needs. Knowing how to support their progress means having some understanding of their varying needs and the skills to know how to help them to become successful learners. Given the range of needs to be found in most classes, this is no small undertaking.

Questions for refection

Think about the educational setting you work in or one you know well:

1. Do you think all teachers see themselves as teachers of pupils who have special needs?
2. If your answer is 'no', how do you think this could improve?
3. If the answer is 'yes', in what ways do they show that this is the case?

Special educational needs co-ordinators (SENCOs)

The key person in arranging support for pupils and, linked to this, the professional development needed by staff in order to provide effective support, is the SEN co-ordinator or SENCO. The post of SENCO was mentioned in the first SEN Code of Practice, which came into force in 1994. By the time the second Code appeared in 2001, the role of the SENCO was well established and its significance beginning to be better understood. As mentioned in Chapter 1 of this book, one of the few changes that was made to the SEN system after the Warnock Report and the 1981 Education Act, and before the major changes in 2014, was to raise the status of SENCOs.

The first of these was the 2008 Regulations that meant the person fulfilling this role has to be a qualified teacher. A year later, the *National Award for SEN Co-ordination* was introduced, meaning that any SENCO appointed since September 2009, has had to undertake this training within three years of taking up the role. The learning outcomes are in three parts:

Part A   Professional knowledge and understanding

Part B   Leading and co-ordinating provision

Part C   Personal and professional qualities.

(Further details can be found in the revised *National Award for SEN Co-ordination: Learning Outcomes*, published in April 2014 by the National College for Teaching and Leadership (NCTL)). At first, only a certain number of Higher Education institutions and other organisations were allowed to offer the Award, but since then the restrictions have been loosened. However, it has become harder to get funding to cover the cost of the training although it remains mandatory.

SENCOs' roles and responsibilities

In the SEN Code, which was in place from 2001 to August 2014, the role of the SENCO was set out in three different chapters: (i) Early Education Settings; (ii) Primary Phase; and (iii) Secondary Sector. In the SEND Code which came in on 1 September 2014, and was re-issued in January 2015, the role is also set out in three chapters, but the division is: Early Years Providers, Schools and Further Education.

Early years

Chapter 5 of the SEND Code of Practice states that maintained nursery schools must have a qualified teacher who is designated as the SENCO. The four bullet points describing the role are set out on page 89, paragraph 5.54. These are:

- Ensuring all practitioners in the setting understand their responsibilities to children with SEN and the setting's approach to identifying and meeting SEN
- Advising and supporting colleagues
- Ensuring parents are closely involved throughout and their insights inform action taken by the setting
- Liaising with professionals or agencies beyond the setting.

There is not the same expectation of early years providers who are not nursery schools. For some of them, the role of the Area SENCO helps to fill the gap and local authorities (LAs) are encouraged to use them. As an Area SENCO is likely to have responsibility for several settings, their brief goes wider than SENCOs in nursery schools. Their remit is set out on pages 89–90 of the Code, paragraph 5.56, but with the proviso that the role will vary depending on the type and number of settings the Area SENCO is covering.

Schools

In chapter 6 of the SEND Code, no distinction is made between the SENCOs working in primary or secondary schools, all of whom are seen as taking on a more strategic and wide-ranging role. In outline, the 11 dimensions of the role are as follows:

- Overseeing the operation of the schools' SEN Policy
- Co-ordinating provision for pupils with SEN
- Liaising with the Designated Teacher if a 'looked after' pupil also has SEN
- Advising on the graduated approach to SEN support
- Advising on how the school's delegated budget and other resources are deployed
- Liaising with parents of pupils with SEN
- Liaising with early years providers, other schools, educational psychologists (EPs), and health and social care professionals
- Being the key contact with external agencies, especially the LA and its support services
- Liaising with the providers of the next stage of a pupil's education and ensuring parents are kept informed about options
- Working with the head teachers and governors to make sure the school meets its responsibilities under the Equality Act (2010)
- Ensuring records of pupils with SEN are kept up to date.

(paragraph 6.90)

Further Education

The introduction to chapter 7 of the Code makes it clear that post-16 education and training covers many different types of provision, including school sixth forms, sixth form colleges, FE colleges, 16–19 academies, special post-16 institutions, as well as vocational learning and various forms of training. However, the chapter concentrates largely on FE colleges, which are not required to have a SENCO as such, but someone undertaking a similar role:

> Colleges should ensure that there is a named person in the college with oversight of SEN provision to ensure co-ordination of support, similar to the role of the SENCO in schools. (paragraph 7.22)

This same paragraph gives an outline, in general terms, of what the role might include. It mentions contributing to strategic and operational management of the college and being the person colleagues can turn to for help in identifying and supporting a student who may have SEN. However, the role is not as clearly defined as in other settings.

Activity for SENCOs

Think about how your role has changed from the 2001 Code of Practice and how you might explain this to your colleagues.

As part of this activity, think about how you might help to clarify for them the difference between the role of the SENCO and the role of other teaching staff in terms of their responsibilities for pupils with SEND and their families.

Early years and SEND

The first case study in this chapter is of an early years setting where a nursery school and a children's centre are on the same site and under the same management.

Key point: Children's centres

Children's centres were established in 2004 in the wake of the Children Act and placed on a statutory footing in 2009, with the aim of helping young children in disadvantaged areas to be better prepared for school. By 2010, the target number of 3,500 children's centres had been reached.

After the government changed hands, there was concern that some children's centres were being closed. In April 2013, the DfE updated the previous guidance, stating that: 'Sure Start children's centres improve outcomes for young children and their families and reduce inequalities, particularly for those families in greatest need of support'.

In June 2014, the DfE said that there were 3,000 children's centres, but argued that this was due to some being amalgamated rather than closed.

Children's centres are run by a number of different providers, including schools. They may be single entities or part of a group.

Case study of a nursery school and children's centre

In 2011, Bedworth Heath Nursery School and Children's Centre was one of a group of six nurseries and children's centres in Warwickshire that were selected by the DfE to form a network of 16 Early Years Teaching Centres across England. The head teacher, Amanda King, believes that a set menu of training is not the right way forward, as any training needs to reflect the individual needs and priorities of different settings. So, the approach of her Early Years Teaching Centre is to have a joint agreement with individual settings about what will be delivered. Any course of training is then followed up in order to evaluate its impact on practice.

Case study 📁

Bedworth Heath Nursery School and Children's Centre

The nursery school provides 80 part-time places for 3- and 4-year-olds, who are admitted in September or January and attend for three or five terms.

The classrooms and outdoor areas, including a forest area, allow for 'free-flow activities', while 'family time' in small groups is used for more focused teaching opportunities. There is a lunch club that either morning or afternoon children can use, where healthy eating is encouraged. Because of the level of development some young children have when they start, the school incorporates a Nurture Nursery for 2-year-olds who need the most support and a different kind of environment.

There is a flexible arrangement about the number of sessions a child attends in the main classes and preference is given to families in receipt of benefits. A quarter of the children have SEN. The school is equipped with facilities for children who have physical disabilities. Staff have experience of supporting children with a wide variety of additional educational and medical needs, including children with severe and complex needs. All children are encouraged to talk about their learning and their likes and dislikes using signs, symbols or verbal communication as appropriate.

Pupils are identified as needing extra support or having SEN through the use of daily observations, weekly assessments and termly tracking in all seven areas of learning of the Early Years Foundation Stage (EYFS) curriculum. Amanda King has devised the school's tracking system, which, along with the EYFS Profile, enables all children's needs to be carefully targeted and tracked. Daily conversations with parents are actively encouraged and they are closely involved with decisions that are made about any extra support their child needs. Parents also contribute to policy development, and newsletters explain how they can be involved at a strategic level, in addition to those who are governors.

The children's centre and childcare provision on the same site means that there are education, care and family services for children and their families covering birth to five. The centre is open all year from 8am to 6pm and on-site 'wrap around' childcare from 8am to 5.30pm is available for 50 weeks of the year to children under 8. There is a sessional nursery for 2–3-year-olds and various Play and Stay sessions parents or carers and their child can attend. Families can also learn about a variety of topics such as: feeding and nutrition; financial matters; health issues; housing; getting jobs; managing behaviour; safety in the home; sleep routines; toilet training; and volunteer placements.

As the school is an Early Years Teaching Centre, staff have to reflect constantly on their own practice, so that they are in a position to work with other nursery schools and children's centres on improving the quality of children's learning experiences. Amanda King says 'Mutual respect and a shared understanding of why quality matters are crucial'. The school works with a wide range of other partners, including: community police; family information services; the Information, Advice and Support Service (IASS), Nuneaton & Bedworth College; George Eliot Hospital; the Integrated Disability Service; the Mental Health Crisis Team; and the NHS Information Service for Parents.

Embedding practice within schools

The next case study is an example that also follows the Nurture group approach for some of its pupils.

Key point: Nurture groups

Nurture groups were developed in 1969 by the educational psychologist, Marjorie Boxall, who was aware of children starting school who were unable to form trusting relationships with other children or with adults, which she put down to a lack of appropriate nurturing in the first three years of life.

Nurture groups were formed, first of all in primary schools, where small groups of children could develop socially and emotionally, by being given some of the basic learning experiences they had missed out on, rather than being expected to be ready for formal learning in a large class.

Today, Nurture groups can be found in a range of different settings, from nursery schools to secondary schools and in special schools and other settings.

A primary school case study

The head teacher of Netherfield Primary School, Sharon Gray, taught for many years in special schools, taking up headships in schools for pupils with behaviour, emotional and social development (BESD), as they were called at the time. Having become experienced at working with pupils whose behaviour could be very challenging or worrying, she was keen to take this experience into a mainstream setting, in order to see whether similar approaches could be made to work there.

Sharon says that she is delighted with the move away from the BESD description in the 2014 SEND Code of Practice to 'social, emotional and mental health difficulties' (SEMH). Firstly, she believes it will encourage people to look behind the behaviour to what is causing it. Secondly, it includes the term 'mental health difficulties' which she feels has not been given sufficient prominence up to now.

Mental health

In June 2014, a month before the July version of the SEND Code of Practice 2014 appeared, the DfE published *Mental Health and Behaviour in Schools: Departmental Advice for School Staff* (2014l), which states that 'one in ten children aged 5 to 16 has a clinically diagnosed mental health disorder and one in seven has less severe problems' (p. 4). It stresses a number of issues including the need to:

- Help pupils to become resilient and mentally healthy
- Look out for early signs of distress and intervene early to strengthen resilience before serious mental health problems occur
- Get support for pupils with more severe problems through Child and Adolescent Mental Health Services (CAMHS), voluntary organisations and local GPs
- Influence the health services that are commissioned locally through their local Health and Wellbeing Board, of which Directors of Children's Services and local Healthwatch are statutory members
- Ensure that young people and their families are involved in any decisions, given relevant information and support, and their views, wishes and feelings are considered

---

Key point: Healthwatch, MindEd and SDQ

Healthwatch England is the national consumer champion for health and social care, with statutory powers to ensure the voice of the consumer is heard by relevant bodies. It consists of Healthwatch England and a local Healthwatch in each of the LAs. To find the local one go to: www.healthwatch.co.uk

MindEd provides information about particular conditions and gives access to free online training tools. Counselling MindEd is another aspect of its work: www.minded.org.uk

Strengths and Difficulties Questionnaire (SDQ) is a brief screening check for 3–16-year-olds which is part of the DfE's 2014 document and includes useful information on different mental health needs.

As the school population has become more complex, mainstream schools have been changing their practice to accommodate this different population.

Case study

Netherfield Primary School, Nottingham

The school has around 490 pupils aged 4 to 11, with the age range being extended to admit 2-year-olds from September 2014. It is open from 8am to 8pm. When Sharon Gray was appointed as the head teacher five years ago, the school had gone through a period of change due to the amalgamation of the Infant and Junior schools. Around 40% of pupils are entitled to free school meals (FSM) and around a quarter have SEN.

There are two nurture classes with eight pupils in each and a 10-place SEN Unit. In line with the 2014 SEND Code of Practice, the school makes sure that pupils are receiving high quality teaching before they are identified as having special needs. The inclusive ethos means that all staff take responsibility for assessing, identifying and responding to pupils' needs. This approach has resulted in the school accepting a number of 'managed moves' from other schools to avoid exclusions. There are counsellors and a therapist on the staff, as well as two full-time home/school liaison workers. Where a child has attachment issues, work is done with the whole family.

The school teaches mood management and pupils are encouraged to talk about how they feel. Peer massage and meditation are seen as other ways of helping pupils to remain calm. Every class has a retreat area, where a child can go to be on their own; a role play area; and a reading area where they can sit quietly with a book.

The school describes its curriculum as a skills-based, creative curriculum, which allows some flexibility for classes and individuals to follow their interests. Each class is seen as a constituency and there is a school Parliament. The school has achieved the Investors in Pupils Award, which is described later on in this chapter. The Head and her staff go out of their way to encourage the involvement of families and the wider community. All staff and several parents help to run the Netherfield University, which is the name for the 50 or so after-school clubs, where children and adults can learn together and gain awards for their studies.

The Job Centre comes into the school once a month and local businesses often inform Sharon when jobs are becoming available. There is a small farm in the grounds which some of the families, particularly dads, help to look after. The whole community is invited in once a year to help plan the next stage of the school's development.

The school is becoming a teaching school in 2015 and Sharon is keen to test out her blueprint for experiential learning, with its emphasis on improving mental health and well-being. She says: 'What we try to do is to find creative ways of removing the barriers that obstruct children's learning'.

Activity

1. Go to the website www.sdqinfo.com and have a look at the SDQ questionnaire. Try using it with one of your pupils or someone you know and then check the results.
2. Discuss the ways in which your setting tries to build up resilience in children.

Embedding practice within schools – secondary

The next case study is of a secondary school that has developed various provisions within it so that it provides different types of support depending on a pupil's needs. The head teacher, Jonathan Fawcett, describes his school as a comprehensive and inclusive secondary school, where pupils can move freely in and out of the different environments within it. In order to give pupils a gradual transition to life in a secondary school, Swanwick appoints a teacher who supports Year 6 pupils who may have difficulty transferring to secondary provision and ensures there are strategies in place to support them before they arrive. These are shared with all class teachers prior to the start of the term. A specialist TA works across cluster schools during the Spring and Summer Terms with these pupils and then supports them when they transfer, spending time during the Autumn Term in their classes and liaising with teachers and parents.

Case study

Swanwick School, Derbyshire

This school is a larger than average comprehensive school with approximately 1275 students aged 11–18, including 180 in the sixth form. A small number of Year 10 and 11 students (about 25% of each cohort) attend courses in hair & beauty, construction or motor vehicle maintenance at Alfreton Vocational Academy, or engineering at TS2000 in Derby, which is an independent training provider. The school has specialist status in Technology and Applied Learning and has been a training school. Almost all pupils speak English as their first language. An average number have special needs or disabilities. The school gives priority to families living in nearby villages, so it is very much a community school.

The school has close links with the primary schools in its cluster, in order to provide a coherent education from 3 to 18. The Year 7 curriculum builds on the primary school experience and focuses on developing personal, learning and thinking skills (PLTS). The school employs a number of learning mentors, including one specifically for inclusion and another who works with disaffected students at key stage 3. In addition, there is a pastoral manager for each year group who liaises with the educational psychology service, the Child and Adolescent Mental Health Service (CAMHS) and other outside agencies.

The school has a few pupils who are wheelchair users and 25 with autism. The provision made for vulnerable pupils includes:

- A student support centre for persistent absentees and those at risk of exclusion
- The LOFT (Learning Opportunities Friendship Team), which is run by specialist teaching assistants and provides a drop-in centre, specifically for those on the autism spectrum

- A multi-sensory room again run by specialist TAs which is known as 'Positive Support'
- An Inclusion Unit which has been running for several years and has helped to reduce exclusions. It also takes pupils when they are being readmitted, or as a preventative strategy. It is housed in a separate building and the pupils have breaks at different times, with the curriculum being taught in the morning and their issues addressed in the afternoon. The school previously had the highest rate of fixed term exclusions in the county and now consistently runs at less than half the national average for all groups of students. No student has been permanently excluded for over four years.

Student voice is a feature of the school. As well as a Student Council which has regular communication with the head and the governors, there are student forums. Students help with the appointment of staff and are given leadership opportunities. The school has gained the 'Investors in Pupils' award (see below).

Jonathan is a firm believer that a strong partnership between students, their parents and the staff is the most effective way of achieving the best outcomes. The school was one of the first to gain the Investors in Pupils award.

Key point: Investors in Pupils

Investors in Pupils builds on the four key principles of Investors in People: commitment, review, action, improvement. At its heart is pupil voice and participation. It helps pupils to find out about their school, the roles of those who work there and how the school runs on a budget. They learn about the school's resources, including the staff who support them.

Pupils set targets for their class and understand how they themselves can make a difference. They develop an awareness of their own role and take greater control of their behaviour and learning. Much of the work for the award takes place in assemblies and in personal, social, citizenship and health education (PSCHE) classes.

Jonathan says he does not see the changes to the SEN Framework as being radical. The school is already using the graduated approach, has strong links with outside specialists and agencies and has an ongoing programme of training for all staff to improve their understanding of pupils with SEND. The school has already found a number of creative ways of including students who have a range of special needs or are vulnerable in other ways. Pupils in his school can move flexibly in and out of different types of support within the school and there are also close links with a special school on the same site. Jonathan describes the changes as evolutionary and requiring tweaking, reviewing and refining the provision they offer. The school's behaviour system already follows the SEND Code of Practice's approach of: ASSESS (through a termly audit); PLAN (a tailored programme of support); DO (follow the programme for six weeks); REVIEW (look at the data to decide the next phase). Jonathan says that one of the main challenges will be to continue to fund the provision and support that is needed and which makes it possible for them to include such a wide range of pupils.

An academy chain

The final case study in this chapter is another secondary school. This time, it is part of the Ormiston Academies Trust (OAT), which is a charity and incorporated company. It was founded in 2008 and sponsors 30 academies, both primary and secondary. Toby Salt, who is the Chief Executive of OAT, sees the advantages of being part of an academy chain as:

- Being able to share talents and ideas across the network
- Collaborating with other academy networks in the UK
- Having a dedicated school improvement team
- Being able to access expertise, such as marketing, PR, finance, ICT and HR at lower costs
- Working with a sponsor who invests in the future of education
- Supporting schools through Ofsted
- Allowing each of its schools to develop a distinctive personality.

Case study

Nicole McCartney, who is the Executive Principal of Ormiston Venture Academy, explains that the school's four watchwords are: ASPIRE, ACHIEVE, CREATE, INNOVATE. She describes the core business of the school as unlocking pupils' potential. The Academy is divided into four colleges, each named after one of the four watchwords and having its own Assistant Principal. When Nicole arrived, she changed the arrangements for pupils with special needs, many of whom had been taught separately for much of the time, to an emphasis on inclusion and personalisation. The school has two strategic partners: Norfolk County Council (NCC) and Gresham's, the independent co-educational school.

Case study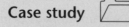

Ormiston Venture Academy, Great Yarmouth

The Academy has around 600 students aged 11–16. It specialises in mathematics and digital media. It opened in new buildings in September 2010, replacing a previous high school. There is a higher than average number of pupils with SEN. All pupils are re-assessed on entry and then every half-term. Pen portraits are used to give a detailed picture of each learner. The school is committed to the creation of a fully inclusive learning community and works closely with its feeder schools to effect a smooth transition for vulnerable pupils.

Provision is made for students with physical disabilities and there is wheelchair access to all areas. Pupils with SEND may have a few lessons outside their classes, for instance in the Success Centre and the Raising Achievement Room, if they need help with literacy, or support for their self-esteem, motivation, organisation, or home learning tasks. This work is supported by high level teaching assistants (HLTAs) and Learning Mentors.

However, the aim is to educate pupils with SEND alongside their peers. This has been made more achievable through the work of the SENDCo in developing comprehensive Strategy Packs giving detailed information about specific needs and strategies for meeting them. In addition, each classroom and every teaching assistant has a personalisation box containing items such as coloured overlays, assorted pens and grips, tangle toys, large calculators, number squares and left handed equipment. Pupils are also encouraged to develop their own cue cards to explain to staff what helps them.

All students are encouraged to voice their opinions and there is a Diary Room where they can record comments of 45 seconds on screen. Some act as peer mentors or councillors. There is a Student Executive Body, with a Student Leadership Structure, as well as Prefects and Captains of Houses. Parents are encouraged to be on committees which consider all aspects of school life, as well as being able to contribute at a strategic level on the Parent Focus Group.

The school has strong relationships with health and social care. Direct referrals can be made to CAMHS, who visit students at the school, while other health professionals have visited to advise on pupils who have ADHD and other conditions. There are links with the nearest special school as well.

At post-16, students are able to move on to a variety of options, including sixth forms in local schools; FE colleges in Great Yarmouth and East Norfolk; or apprenticeships offered by Norfolk CC and local firms.

Out of academy hours, the buildings are used by a mixture of staff and former and present students and their families, as well as the wider community, who learn together, either in private study or through the many clubs that take place.

As regards the changes to the SEN Framework, the academy is happy with the change to SEN Support, but, within this, prefers to talk in terms of Wave 1 and Wave 2 pupils, depending on whether or not they have a statement or EHC Plan. They have used the 'Assess, Plan, Do, Review' approach for some time in preference to IEPs. The school finalised its SEN Information Report before the deadline of September 2014 and has used this as its contribution to the LA's Local Offer. In addition, the school has developed a booklet for parents and carers, which gives a fuller account of the school's approach to special needs. The school has a separate SEND Policy.

Inclusion takes many forms

This chapter has looked at the practices used by some mainstream settings to include a much broader range of pupils than schools may have been used to. The variety of ways in which children and young people are supported illustrates that there is no one right way of meeting their needs, because every setting and every child is unique. What the settings have in common is a determination to enable every pupil to be included in the life of the school, and to personalise pupils' learning experiences, so that they gain the skills they will need both now and in the future.

The next chapter looks at how those working in specialist and alternative provision are also finding ways of making sure every pupil, however complex their needs, is able to participate in, and benefit fully from, their experience of school.

Further reading

For additional information, you can refer to the relevant sections of the SEND Code of Practice 2015:
SEND Code of Practice 2015: Chapter 5 (Early Years), chapter 6 (Schools), or chapter 7 (Further Education), plus Annex 1 on Mental Capacity.

Cheminais, R. (2014) *Rita Cheminais' Handbook for SENCOs*, 2nd edn. London: Sage.
DfE (2014l) *Mental Health and Behaviour in Schools: Departmental Advice for School Staff.* Department for Education.
NCTL (2014) *National Award for SEN Co-ordination: Learning Outcomes.* National College for Teaching and Leadership.
Tutt, R. and Williams, P. (2012) *How Successful Schools Work: The Impact of Innovative School Leadership.* London: Sage.

Meeting SEN in specialist and alternative provision

Chapter overview

This chapter considers how different types of specialist and alternative provision address the needs of pupils for whom learning creates a significant challenge.

There is a consideration of the change in the SEND Code of Practice from Behaviour, Emotional and Social Development (BESD) to Social, Emotional and Mental Health Difficulties (SEMH) and case studies of a non-maintained and a free school for these pupils.

The chapter also covers the overlap between pupils with these needs and pupils who find themselves in various types of Alternative Provision (AP), as both are inclined to arrive with a history of being excluded or at risk of exclusion.

The steps that have been taken to give both young learners and their families a more strategic role are considered through a case study of a large special school and a snapshot of a school that has been successful in engaging 'hard to reach' parents.

The chapter ends with two case studies of AP free schools, both supported by head teachers, one of which is a Multi-Academy Trust (MAT).

Specialist and alternative provision

Whereas the previous chapter considered different approaches to meeting needs in mainstream schools, the present chapter looks at the role played by various forms of specialist and alternative provision.

Replacing the term 'BESD' with 'SEMH'

As was mentioned previously in this book, three of the four broad areas of need in the current SEND Code of Practice have stayed the same as they were in the 2001 version. The one change was to 'behavioural, emotional and social development' (BESD). When the first draft of what became the 2015 SEND Code appeared in October 2013, the term used was 'social, mental and emotional health'. Concern was expressed that the word 'mental' stood out in an unhelpful way and so it was moved to attach it to 'mental health'.

This was a time when there was a growing recognition that children and young people who have special needs are more at risk of developing mental health difficulties. The reason given for the disappearance in the Code of the word 'behaviour' is that, as a term it is not particularly useful. What is more important is the need to look underneath the behaviour at why someone is behaving in a certain way:

> These behaviours may reflect underlying mental health difficulties such as anxiety or depression, self-harming, substance misuse, eating disorders or physical symptoms that are medically unexplained. Other children and young people may have disorders such as attention deficit disorder, attention deficit hyperactivity disorder or attachment disorder. (paragraph 6.32)

A school for emotional and social difficulties

The first case study in this chapter is of Muntham House in West Sussex, which is one of 70 non-maintained special schools in the UK. The Principal, Richard Boyle, says that over the last ten years or so, he has seen a considerable change in his pupil population. Before, he had pupils with less complex needs, who were academically able and who responded quite quickly to finding themselves in an environment where they felt safe. Today, students have more complex needs, including mental health problems, that take time to address. Richard is pleased that 'behaviour' has disappeared from the description of need and sees his school as being for boys who have emotional and social needs. In discussing the overlap between pupils referred to his school and those who are admitted to pupil referral units (PRUs), he says that it is not always a clear distinction, as both take pupils with a history of exclusions. However, where their needs are very complex and require a longer-term solution, he feels that a boarding and day school with a range of therapeutic approaches, may be more appropriate in meeting pupils' entrenched difficulties. One of the awards the school has received is the Investors in Careers Award.

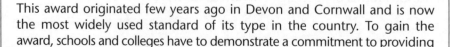

Key point: Investors in Careers

This award originated few years ago in Devon and Cornwall and is now the most widely used standard of its type in the country. To gain the award, schools and colleges have to demonstrate a commitment to providing impartial, independent careers advice and guidance to all young people. Primary, secondary and special schools, FE colleges, special FE colleges and training providers are all eligible for the award.

Website: www.investorincareers.org.uk

Case study

Muntham House, W. Sussex

Muntham House is a boarding and day schools for 60 boys aged 8–19 who have social and emotional difficulties. Many are on the autism spectrum. The school has specialist status for BESD and is used by 20 different local authorities (LAs). The school aims to create a safe, happy and caring environment within which pupils create new behaviours which enable them to be successful in moving forward.

Due to the complex nature of the students' needs, the school uses a number of therapeutic interventions which include: various types of counselling, cognitive behavioural therapy (CBT), art therapy, drama therapy, drum therapy, sound therapy, horsemanship and equine therapy, and family therapy, as well as positive touch and massage, the emotional freedom technique, crisis intervention, nurture groups, behaviour management and restorative justice.

Staff who are new to the school are given a one-year induction programme and all teaching staff have 21 days INSET each year rather than five. This is achieved by using long weekends. There is an emphasis on applied learning and from the age of 14, there are various options, so that students can prepare for apprenticeships, FE or University as appropriate. The school has twice received the Investors in Careers Award.

Although the boys often have a poor attendance record, it improves when they start to enjoy coming to school. The work of the Family Inclusion Team is having very positive results for both the school and the families it supports. The school has many links with schools and colleges in the locality, as well as further afield and has been running courses for a number of years.

Although the age range goes up to 19, some students continue until 21, if they need longer before they are ready to move full-time to college or a work environment. Richard says that one of the difficulties is that it often takes at least three years of disrupted education, during which time pupils may be moved from school to school, or excluded a number of times, before they arrive at Muntham House. He is concerned whether the changes to the SEN Framework will really result in earlier intervention for some of the most emotionally disturbed pupils.

Certainly, one of the intentions of the 2014 SEND Code of Practice is that children and young people's needs should be addressed as soon as they start to emerge. With a greater focus on SEN across the services, and with children and families playing a bigger part in how needs are addressed, it is to be hoped that early intervention, which has always been recognised as the key, will become more of a reality.

Questions for reflection

1. Go back to the list of therapies and approaches that the school in the previous case study uses and look up any that are not familiar to you.
2. What therapies, approaches or interventions does your school or setting use to support pupils with SEN?
3. Are there additional ones that might be beneficial and, if so, would they require specialist staff or additional funding?

An all-age special academy

The second case study in this chapter is Bradfields Academy, which is a specialist provision covering a wide range of age phases and needs. In particular, the case study demonstrates some of the ways in which schools are giving a broader role to the pupils and parents in their school community. In common with other special schools/academies today, it does not work in isolation from the wider community and the Principal, Kim Johnson, has worked with two fellow head teachers to establish a free school. This is given as a separate case study later in the chapter (Inspire Free School), and follows on from the point that was made earlier about the overlap between schools for pupils with emotional and social difficulties and PRUs.

Case study

Bradfields Academy, Medway

Bradfields Academy is a large 4–19 specialist provision with nearly 300 pupils. It became an academy in April 2014. The academy has more than 120 pupils with a pure diagnosis of autism, the rest having severe learning difficulties (SLD) and moderate learning difficulties (MLD). Kim Johnson refers to the population as having complex needs. The academy has an off-site suite of rooms in the nearby Strood Academy, for pupils who are capable of accessing the lower levels of the national curriculum when they reach Year 7. When they have made suitable progress they will be able to transfer from Bradfields to Strood Academy. For older pupils, Bradfields uses alternative vocational courses off-site at Mid Kent College,

Hadlow College and the Catch 22 provision for small groups of key stage 4 and sixth form students. (Catch 22 is a social business that aims to transform lives and communities).

The academy is organised into five learning zones:

- Blue Zone (EYFS to KS5 autism with SLD/MLD)
- Yellow Zone (KS3 SLD/ MLD)
- Red Zone (KS4 SLD / MLD)
- Green Zone (KS5 SLD / MLD)
- Bradfields@Strood Academy (KS3 MLD)

In addition to the Parent Teachers and Friends Association (PTFA), there is a Parent/Carer Partnership Consultative Group which helps to evaluate and contribute to the academy's policies. The academy has achieved the Leading Parent Partnership Award (LPPA) and was the first school/academy to be awarded the Family Friendly Schools UK Certificate of Accreditation, which is run by the Family and Childcare Trust and awarded to a wide variety of organisations.

As well as a Student Council, there are Student Consultative Groups which look at different elements of the academy's work and are involved in staff appointments. Some pupils act as Student Detectives who are tasked with identifying positive behaviour as well as that requiring change. There are Student Mentors who assist staff on duty and two Youth Commissioners who help the LA with policies and are paid for their work. The academy has the Investors in Pupils Award, which was described in the previous chapter.

Key point: Leading Parent Partnership Award (LPPA)

This is a national award that supports effective parental engagement. It is run by Prospects, which is the largest provider of the Connexions service to schools (which provides careers guidance). It has been running since 2003, with over 800 educational establishments having taken part. There are three ways of achieving the Award:

- Route 1: An adviser works with the school throughout and produces an Action Plan
- Route 2: Although a trainer works with the school, it does its own Action Plan
- Route 3: The setting uses the toolkit and materials without support.

Once achieved, the award is reassessed every three years.

Reaching all parents and carers

Another school that has been particularly active in involving parents, including those who may be reluctant to engage with the school, is Selworthy School, which is a Specialist Centre for Cognition and Learning in Somerset. The head teacher, Karen Milton, established a FAST Team when the changes to the SEN Framework were still being discussed.

Case study

Selworthy Special School's FAST Team

FAST stands for **F**amilies **a**nd **S**chool **T**ogether. It began as a project in November 2012 and, due to its success, has continued to be a part of the school's work. As well as encouraging all parents and carers to feel involved and included, there has been a particular focus on developing relationships with those who traditionally do not engage with the school.

The Team has a base where people can meet in a relaxed atmosphere. Individual concerns can be addressed and practical help given on various issues, such as: explaining about sources of funding and what personal budgets and direct payments mean; helping parents to complete forms or get in touch with other agencies; supporting those who want to become confident with electronic devices.

The secret of the Team's success and its ability to reach all parents, may be down to the fact that it is run by parents for parents. A team of three parents is employed by the school to find ways of helping parents and carers to engage with the school and to play a bigger part in supporting their children's learning and development.

A free school for social and emotional difficulties

The next case study, which was referred to earlier, is the result of the work of three local head teachers, Medway Council and the Williamson Trust, to open a free school for the most vulnerable secondary pupils in the area, in terms of their emotional and social needs. In addition to Kim Johnson (mentioned previously), the other two head teachers involved are Dr Gary Holden, the head of a grammar school (Sir Joseph Williamson Mathematical Academy) and Chief Education Officer (CEO) of The Williamson Trust, and Andy Reese, head teacher of Greenacre Academy, a sports college which supports the Walderslade network of schools.

Although Medway has many forms of specialist provision, there was a lack of full-time BESD/SEMH provision for pupils of secondary age. The free school was designed to address this gap, and, at the same time, extend opportunities for older pupils. This is particularly important in the light of

Raising the Participation Age (RPA), which means that young people have to: continue in full-time education; have an apprenticeship or traineeship; or receive part-time education combined with being employed or volunteering, for 20 or more hours a week until the age of 18. The new school hopes that it will help school leavers to avoid becoming NEETs (Not in Employment, Education, or Training).

Case study

Inspire Free School

The school opened in September 2014 with 40 pupils, who had previously been at a PRU but whose main need was thought to be their social and emotional difficulties. It is intended to grow to a maximum of 80 students (boys and girls) aged 11–19.

The decision was made in the light of the changes to the SEN system and the SEND Code of Practice 2015, which raised concerns about the education of young people whose behaviour arises from their emotional, social or mental health needs and who require a different style of education from that used in PRUs. This new school recognises that the most challenging students may require long-term, therapeutic support, rather than being reintegrated in the shorter term (if at all), or having part-time provision.

Although most of the students will have EHC Plans before they arrive, as a special free school, assessment placements can also be arranged, in order to meet needs as soon as their severity becomes apparent, rather than wait for a Plan to be completed. The school commissions the services parents want for their children through a close partnership with them and with health, care and education.

A post-16 programme is being developed, which will be individualised for each learner and the school will provide additional pathways to learning for students who, at 16, are not ready to sustain a placement at college. The post-16 provision will be commissioned in partnership with local colleges, businesses and other schools, in order to maximise the opportunities for each learner.

The Free School is working in tandem with partner agencies: health and social care colleagues; the Medway Youth Trust; and the police.

Pupil referral units (PRUs) and Alternative Provision (AP)

Pupil referral units (PRUs) are one of the main forms of alternative provision. They teach children who are not able to attend school and may not otherwise receive a suitable education. The main reason for their attendance at a PRU is because they have been excluded or are at risk of exclusion.

However, some PRUs also accept pupils who need a place for other reasons, such as while waiting for a school place to become available, having a medical condition, or being a school refuser. What is seldom mentioned is that many students who are on the roll of a PRU also attend additional forms of alternative provision off site.

Children in PRUs and AP are twice as likely as the average pupil to qualify for free school meals. They are more likely to have had poor attendance in school and to be known to social services and sometimes to the police as well. A large majority of pupils in PRUs have SEN, but, as noted earlier, the boundaries between AP and SEN provision are blurred. In addition, it should be noted that two-thirds of pupils in AP, including PRUs, are boys. There is a broad range of provision on offer, from therapeutic independent schools for children with severe behavioural, emotional and social development (BESD) to small local providers offering training, for example in car maintenance, for one or two pupils. Providers of AP include FE colleges, charities, businesses and independent schools, as well as the public sector.

Developments in PRUs and other forms of AP

From 2011 to 2014, the DfE ran a trial in which schools retained responsibility and funding for the education of pupils they permanently exclude. Some LAs had already developed this model, where schools have the opportunity to use the money more creatively to provide bespoke interventions for individual pupils.

In 2013 the DfE established a reference group to look at alternative provision. The group has continued to meet throughout 2014 and beyond, in order to:

- Contribute to alternative provision policy development and implementation
- Develop clearer measures of success by identifying good practice for AP providers
- Support the creation of AP academies, through conversion, sponsorship or intervention
- Encourage AP free schools, and other models of delivery
- Support a more significant role for PRUs (and, in time, AP Academies) in teacher training.

Case studies of Alternative Provision (AP)

As part of its academisation programme, the Coalition Government was keen to see PRUs convert to academy status and by September 2014, there were 36 either open or approved to open. The change became evident when the national organisation for PRUs became PRUsAP (the National Organisation for PRUs and Alternative Providers in England and Wales).

The final two case studies are of newer types of provision. The first is an AP Academy set up by a group of secondary schools known as the Harrow Collegiate. The second is a group of AP academies within the Tri-borough LAs of Hammersmith & Fulham, Kensington & Chelsea and Westminster, which has been established under a Multi-Academy Trust (MAT).

Harrow Collegiate is an example of a number of secondary schools across a town or area coming together to provide a wider range of exam subjects than is possible for a single school to deliver on its own. The Collegiate has also opened an AP free school, known as Jubilee Academy.

Case study

Jubilee Academy, Harrow

The Jubilee Academy opened in September 2013. It provides for students aged 11–16 and offers both short- and long-term placements for pupils needing a smaller-school experience, a more personalised curriculum, and a different experience of learning to overcome any barriers they may have. Groups are based on pupils' ability and lessons last for 50 minutes, with occasional double lessons.

The curriculum is progression related and focuses on transferable skills, including workplace learning. It is designed to be interesting by securing community involvement and exploration. It is personalised and able to be flexible in order to address students' needs, including their self-esteem, self-awareness and self-confidence.

At KS3, there is an emphasis on the core subjects of English, Maths and Science. At KS4 all students study for GCSEs in English, English Literature, Science and Maths. They can also study for a range of vocational qualifications.

An extensive out-of-hours programme called 'Beyond the Classroom' brings additional enrichment opportunities and all students are encouraged to take part. They range from The Jubilee Drama Academy and the Art Stop, to Duke of Edinburgh Awards and the Survival of the Fittest.

The TBAP (Tri-borough Alternative Provision)

This was established as a Multi-Academy Trust (MAT) in March 2013, and is an approved DfE Academy sponsor. It is led by Seamus Oates, Executive Head Teacher of the Bridge AP Academy, which he opened 13 years ago. As Seamus explained in an article for *The Guardian*, they don't view the students as victims, but they do clearly see mitigating circumstances that explain their difficult behaviour: 'With every learner there is a story that explains why they are here. Not an excuse, but a story. I feel very moved when I see the kids coming in who still want to learn. Usually they have been let down by an adult'.

> ## Case study 📁
>
> ### (TBAP) Tri-borough Alternative Provision
>
> The AP academies and services that make up TBAP are:
>
> - Bridge AP Academy
> - Courtyard AP Academy
> - Beachcroft AP Academy
> - Latimer AP Academy
> - Octagon AP Academy
> - Commissioning and School Support.
>
> TBAP aims to ensure a safe and stimulating learning environment across its provisions, using robust systems of behaviour and pastoral support to deliver effective well-being for all its students. The Trust tries to provide the most effective, time-limited support as quickly and as flexibly as possible.
>
> The provisions use a highly personalised curriculum, 21st-century learning spaces, knowledgeable practitioners and therapeutic interventions to ensure the rapid progress of learners and to raise their achievement and aspirations. Robust data are used to provide interventions that narrow the gap, deliver reintegration, and are used in the quest for delivering academic, social and emotional learning, which enables learners to become successful and thoughtful lifelong learners, respectful of others' viewpoints and ideas. TBAP offers an entitlement of a minimum of five GCSEs or equivalent in the secondary phase.
>
> One of the students said: 'Life at this school is much calmer. The classes are smaller, and there's more help. At my last school there was a counsellor who came every two weeks. Here there are counsellors present all the time'.

The next chapter moves on to look at the importance of workforce development, which must go hand in glove with the improvements that the SEND Code of Practice is designed to bring about. If every teacher is a teacher of special needs, then from initial teacher training (ITT) onwards, a carefully planned programme of continuing professional development (CPD) for staff across settings should be a key factor in enabling them to fulfil that role.

Further reading

For additional information, you can refer to the relevant sections of the SEND Code of Practice 2015:
SEND Code of Practice 2015: Chapter 10 – Children and young people in specific circumstances and chapter 11 – Resolving disagreements.

Cheminais, R. (2011) *Family Partnership Working: A Guide for Education Practitioners*. London: Sage.

DfE (2011b) *Improving Alternative Provision: Charlie Taylor, The Government's Expert Adviser on Behaviour*. London: HMSO.

DfE (2014m) *School Exclusion Trial Evaluation: Research Report*. Department for Education.

Ofsted (2011) *Alternative Provision Survey*. Manchester: Ofsted Publications.

Developing the workforce

Chapter overview

This chapter traces the interest in better training for all staff from the Lamb Inquiry onwards, as well as approaches to school improvement. It covers the various routes into ITT and their SEND components, as well as mandatory qualifications for teachers who have QTS (qualified teacher status).

    The move to school-based ITT is traced and there are examples of two of the schools mentioned in previous chapters which are teaching schools.

    The chapter ends by highlighting some of the important resources listed in Annex 2 of the SEND Code of Practice, which will help professionals keep on top of developments in the field of SEND, and the online and other training opportunities that can contribute substantially to CPD (continuing professional development).

The background

In recent years, there has been a shift to move much of ITT (initial teacher training) from university departments into schools. Although universities remain involved, it is through schools linking with them rather than the other way round. With a plethora of possible routes into teaching, concern has grown about how well all trainee teachers are prepared to teach children and young people who have SEND. This has been thrown into sharp relief by the requirement in the SEND Code of Practice 2015 that emphasises every teacher, whatever their role, is a teacher of pupils who have special needs and is responsible for their progress.

As mentioned in the opening chapter, one of the reports that served as a background to the 2014 changes to the SEN framework was the *Lamb Inquiry: Special Educational Needs and Parental Confidence* (DCSF, 2009). In it, Brian Lamb pointed out that parents would have greater confidence in the system if they felt that staff were better trained:

> The overwhelming message from parents is of the value they place on staff with the skills and expertise to enable their child to learn and progress: someone who understands my child's needs. (paragraph 2.32)

This is not a criticism of professionals, but of the way their training has rarely paid enough attention to the fifth or so of the population who have SEN in the longer or shorter term. From initial teacher training (ITT) onwards, there has been a lack of consistency and coherence about how much time is spent on this important aspect of training.

The training and development of staff

Although the training and professional development of staff goes wider than school staff, the emphasis in this chapter is on staff in early years, schools and post-16 provision. However, it should be mentioned that some local authorities (LAs) have been active in retraining staff to develop the skills needed to work with families face to face, rather than dealing with them largely through paperwork. An example of this approach was given in the case study of the Hertfordshire SEND Pathfinder in Chapter 5.

And, of course, the changes to the SEN system affect health and social care staff as well, who, as mentioned in the first chapter of this book, have their own guidance documents from the Department for Education (DfE) and the Department of Health (DoH). The one for health professionals (DfE/DoH, 2014d) outlines a role for a Designated Medical Officer (DMO) or a Designated Clinical Officer (DCO), depending on the status of the person undertaking the role. This is someone who will support clinical commissioning groups (CCGs) in meeting their statutory responsibilities and be a point of contact with other partners, including the LA, schools and colleges, in regard to meeting children and young people's health and medical needs.

Teacher training

All initial teacher training (ITT) courses are meant to ensure that any teacher recommended for the award of qualified teacher status (QTS) at the end of the course, must have met all the standards for achieving that status.

Teacher standards

The standards for teachers were revised in 2013 and have been used subsequently as part of the performance management of teachers. The section on 'Adapting teaching to respond to the strengths and needs of all pupils' states that teachers need to:

- Know when and how to differentiate appropriately, using approaches which enable pupils to be taught effectively
- Have a secure understanding of how a range of factors can inhibit pupils' ability to learn, and how best to overcome these
- Demonstrate an awareness of the physical, social and intellectual development of children, and know how to adapt teaching to support pupils' education at different stages of development
- Have a clear understanding of the needs of all pupils – including those with special educational needs, those of high ability, those with English as an additional language, those with disabilities – and to be able to use and evaluate distinctive teaching approaches to engage and support them.

However, with the proliferation of routes into ITT and the variety of course providers, how much time is spent on SEND and exactly what is covered will vary. In May 2014, the government established an *Independent Review of Initial Teachers Training Courses* under the chairmanship of Sir Andrew Carter, head teacher of South Farnham School, which leads the Surrey South Farnham SCITT (School-centred ITT). Its remit was to look at the quality and effectiveness of ITT courses.

Carter Review

The review was published in January 2015, (*Carter review of initial teacher training*, DfE 2015a), at the same time as the government's response to it, (*Government response to the Carter review of initial teacher training (ITT)* (DfE 2015b)). Recommendation 1 was that there should be a core framework common to all ITT courses. This would include:

- Managing pupil behaviour
- Special educational needs
- Child and adolescent development.

In its response, the DfE agreed to establish an independent working group to develop a framework which would ensure all the ITT courses included these three elements. Recommendation 10 said that, wherever possible, there should be placements in special schools, or mainstream schools with resourced provision. Many will welcome the recognition of the importance of all teachers knowing about typical child development, as a basis for understanding how to recognise and support children and young people with a range of different needs, as well as the emphasis on the value of specialist placements.

Mandatory SEND qualifications

At present, there are two types of mandatory qualifications in the area of SEN. In both cases, they are for qualified teachers holding either QTS or QTLS (Qualified Teacher Learning and Skills), which, since April 2012, have had the same status.

1. **National Award for Special Educational Needs Co-ordination**. As mentioned earlier in the book, in September 2009, it became law for every new SENCO in a mainstream school to gain this Masters-level award within three years of taking up the post. It is one of the duties of governing bodies of maintained mainstream schools and proprietors of academy schools to ensure that there is a qualified teacher who holds the post of SENCO. The award has three main parts:

    i. The professional knowledge and understanding that SENCOs need of the legislative context for SEN and theoretical concepts that underpin effective leadership and practice
    ii. The expertise and capabilities that SENCOs need to coordinate and lead provision
    iii. The personal and professional qualities that SENCOs need to make a positive impact on the ethos and culture in schools and other settings.

    The learning outcomes were revised in 2014 in line with the SEND Code of Practice's emphasis on the strategic role that SENCOs are expected to fulfil.

2. **Mandatory training for teaching pupils with sensory impairments.**

    Those who wish to teach children or young people with sensory impairments must take an additional qualification within three years of being in post. During 2013–14, the specifications were slightly revised to bring them in line with the SEND Code of Practice 2015 and other changes that had occurred.

Key point: Mandatory qualifications for sensory impairments

The three mandatory qualifications are as follows:

- Teachers of children and young people who have hearing impairments (HI)
- Teachers of children and young people who have visual impairments (VI)
- Teachers of children and young people who are deafblind

NB 'Deafblind' is the term that has generally replaced multi-sensory impairments (MSI).

Training routes for ITT

The main choice today is between school-based or university-based training and, once this choice has been made, which of a number of courses to pursue. As regards school-based courses, the main route has been the rapid development of 600 teaching schools, with the numbers continuing to rise. Although there is much to be said for a school-led system, the knock-on effect on universities has meant that there are serious concerns about how many will be able to continue to be able to train those who prefer a Higher Education route to QTS.

Both universities and schools offer PGCE (postgraduate certificate in education) for those who already have degrees.

Teaching schools

To be designated a teaching school a school must have been judged outstanding by Ofsted, have consistently outstanding results, and have demonstrated a history of collaboration with other schools. With the largest number at the top, these are the types of schools that have taken on this work to date:

Secondary academies	185
Primary schools	178
Primary academies	94
Secondary schools	47
Special schools	42
Nursery schools	19
Special academies	12
Independent schools	4
Post-16 provision	4
City technology colleges (CTCs)	2
PRUs	2
PRU academies	1

Every teaching school has an alliance of schools it works with and between them they have to deliver all six elements of the role. These are:

1. Initial teacher training (ITT)
2. Continuing professional development (CPD)
3. School-to-school support
4. Identifying and developing leadership potential
5. Specialist leaders of education (SLEs)
6. Research and development.

While the teaching school leads the alliance and organises how the six elements will be covered, it may also have other strategic partners who come from HE, LAs, Academy Chains, Dioceses or organisations from the private sector. Lampton School, which was featured in Chapter 4 of this book, had been a training school before becoming a teaching school in the first tranche in 2011. Because of its expertise, the school enables trainee teachers who wish to do so to specialise in SEN or in English as an Additional Language (EAL).

Case study 📁

Lampton School

The school offers placements to trainees wishing to train on the PGCE route. It provides:

- A fully equipped room set aside for their use
- A trained mentor
- Work in a 'training department' – all departments in the school offer placements every year
- Training in all areas of pedagogy with the opportunity to specialise in teaching students with EAL, SEN or BESD and to learn from outstanding practitioners in these areas, as well as in subjects.

The school is part of the South West London Teachers Education Consortium (SWELTEC), which includes: Brunel University, Institute of Education, Kingston University, London Metropolitan University, Roehampton University and St Mary's University, Twickenham.

Lampton also leads The London West Alliance, which is made up of 20 primary and secondary schools offering School Direct placements, in conjunction with its HE partners, Roehampton University and Goldsmiths, University of London.

Both Lampton and Woodfield School (which was a case study in Chapter 5 and is also a teaching school), are Senior Partners and hub leaders in Challenge Partners, (see under 'Leading school improvement' below). This grew out of the London Challenge, which was established in 2003 to tackle underperformance in the city's schools, through creating effective partnerships between schools, enabling a close focus on the quality of leadership and on the quality of teaching and learning.

Like Lampton, which had been involved in teacher training before becoming a teaching school, Whitefield (which was mentioned in Chapters 4 and 6), has also had a long history of being engaged in the training of teachers before becoming a teaching school in April 2012.

As mentioned in Chapter 4, the school has joined with Joseph Clarke School, which is also a teaching school, to form a Multi-Academy Trust (MAT) under the Whitefield Academy Trust.

Case study

Whitefield Schools and Centre

The school offers a variety of courses, many in collaboration with Kingston University and the University of East London, designed for teaching assistants, all the way to MA programmes for experienced practitioners.

The *School Direct* programme works in partnership with the University of East London. The primary programme focuses on SEN and placements are offered in SEN and mainstream settings. There are both salaried and unsalaried routes.

Run in partnership with Kingston University, Foundation Degrees include an Early Years Foundation Degree for those with some experience of working with babies and children from birth to 5 years old, within an early years setting.

Special Educational Needs and Inclusive Practice is a degree specifically designed for professionals working with children and young people in educational settings who have additional learning needs.

Certificate, Diploma and Masters programmes are delivered in partnership with Kingston University, London. For the diploma, students must be working with pupils who have autism or complex needs.

As well as these training opportunities, Whitefield has a Research and Resource centre that other schools and LAs can buy into.

Leading school improvement

In the same way that the locus of teacher training has shifted to schools, so have school improvement services, which is another aspect of a self-improving, school-led system.

Key point: The Challenge Partnership (CP)

Challenge Partners is a collaborative of over 250 autonomous schools and academies. It is based on the same principles as teaching school alliances, whereby groups of schools work together to lead school improvement. The partnership operates throughout England and includes both mainstream and special schools. Members commit to:

- Increasing students' performance
- Creating more outstanding schools

(Continued)

(Continued)

- Enabling all schools to improve
- Developing a world-class, self-improving and sustainable system

An annual review, on the lines of an Ofsted inspection, takes place by senior leaders of all the schools in the partnership.

Website: http://www.challengepartners.org/

This kind of approach is seen by many as being more effective than an inspection regime, where inspectors deliver their verdict and then may have no further contact with the school. In addition, it has the added advantage of spanning across the phases and sectors of education, thus bringing a wealth of expertise together.

Another aspect of school-led improvement is through the work of national leaders of education (NLEs), local leaders of education (LLEs), specialist leaders of education (SLEs) and NLGs (national leaders of governance). Overseeing the work of LLEs, offering school-to-school support, and developing leadership potential are all part of a teaching school's role.

Key point: NLEs, LLEs, SLEs and NLGs

NLEs and NSS   Head teachers of outstanding schools can apply to become NLEs and the school becomes a national support school (NSS), as the school as a whole is involved with increasing the leadership capacity in other schools as part of raising standards.

LLEs   In this context, head teachers coach or mentor members of leadership teams at other schools in the locality.

SLEs   This gives a similar role to outstanding middle and senior leaders.

NLGs   These are drawn from chairs of governors, who are able to support less experienced chairs.

Involvement of other schools

Many schools that are not themselves teaching schools, belong to teaching school alliances and also contribute in other ways to moving schools forward. Sometimes this will be as part of formal partnerships and sometimes it will be through developments of their own. For instance, a provision that has not been mentioned so far is Shaftesbury High School, which is a special school for a range of needs. Although not a teaching school itself, it belongs to two teaching school alliances and is a National Support School. It has the Investors in People Gold Award for its support for staff development. This has included: running accredited courses for teaching assistants; developing a PGCE course for students who wish to teach in special schools; and creating a taught Masters course, both of the latter in conjunction with the University of East London. The school is a national training provider of CALM (Crisis, aggression, limitation and management) training and has staff who are Elklan-accredited trainers to support speech, communication and language provision.

Continuing professional development

Annex 2 of the SEND Code of Practice 2014 is headed 'Improving Practice and Staff Training in Education Settings'. Although quite brief, it provides a number of very useful links to some of the sources of support, information and training that have become available in the field of SEND.

The main port of call for those wanting to keep up to date and to improve their knowledge, is the SEND Gateway, which has been produced by Nasen (National Association for SEN) with a grant from the DfE. At its launch in May 2014, Edward Timpson, the minister whose brief includes SEN, said that it would become 'A terrific resource for professionals working with those who have SEN'. He went on to explain how it is expected to grow over time. Rather like the Local Offer for parents, the SEND Gateway is a means of gathering together in one place many of the information, resources and training opportunities which professionals are likely to need.

Activity

Go to www.sendgateway.org.uk/ and explore this online information portal by dipping into each of the main areas.

- Select which area is of most interest to you at the moment and start exploring the scope of what is there.
- Jot down anything you would like to explore in greater depth at a later stage.
- Make a note of any materials or information you think would be of benefit or interest to colleagues.

Online training

As the complexity of children's needs increases, the more essential it becomes for staff to understand how to adapt the curriculum and the environment to provide more personalised pathways for pupils who need them. Happily, there is a growing number of training courses and sources of support available. Chief amongst these are online training materials.

The Inclusion Development Programme (IDP): This is an early example of online learning. When it first came out in 2008, it was far from user-friendly. However, all the strands have now been refreshed making it a very useful resource. It covers modules on Speech, Language and Communication Needs (SLCN), Dyslexia, BESD (behavioural, emotional and social development) and autism.

The Lamb materials: This is the first of two more recent resources that are extremely simple to explore, yet contain a wealth of information. The first of these originates from Brian Lamb's report, the *Lamb Inquiry: Special Educational Needs and Parental Confidence* (DCSF, 2009), which has been mentioned previously. His recommendation that staff needed to be better trained to support pupils with SEN, resulted in materials set at Masters level covering the five areas Lamb felt it was most essential for teachers to know about, namely:

- Autism
- Moderate learning difficulties (MLD)
- Behaviour, emotional and social development (BESD)
- Specific learning difficulties (SpLD)
- Speech, language and communication needs (SLCN)

The Complex Needs materials: The second major resource originated from the *Salt Review* (DCSF, 2010), looking at improving the supply of teachers for pupils with SLD (severe learning difficulties) and PMLD (profound and multiple learning difficulties). Also feeding into the materials was the work of The Complex Learning Difficulties and Disabilities (CLDD) Research Project (2009–2011) led by Barry Carpenter. Each of the 16 modules is set at four levels, so there is something to suit everyone.

Both these online materials are designed to be interactive and include activities, video and audio clips of effective practice, links to websites and a wealth of practical resources that can be printed off and used.

The three Trusts

Also mentioned in Annex 2 is the work of the three Trusts which were established in 2010. They are sources of information, resources, support and training in particular areas of SEN. They can be found on their own websites or via the SEND Gateway. They are:

- Autism Education Trust (AET) (www.autismeducationtrust.org.uk)
- The Communication Trust (www.thecommunicationtrust.org.uk)
- The Dyslexia-SpLD Trust (www.thedyslexia-spldtrust.org.uk).

They are well worth exploring as they bring together the work of a range of organisations, and their websites, like the Gateway itself, are constantly updated. The AET has already trained thousands of school staff through its training hubs for early years, schools and post-16 providers, while both the other Trusts provide a wealth of information on the different strategies that have been used as interventions with children who have communication needs or specific learning difficulties. Find out what is there, including the free, downloadable resources.

Going forward

As all teachers are to see themselves as teachers of all the pupils in their classes, including those who have special education needs, it is to be hoped that the Carter Review will help to ensure that every route gives the necessary time and attention to understanding SEND. Beyond that, there needs to be an exploration of how to make sense of the various courses in the field, so that there is a clear path to gaining additional qualifications.

Further reading

For additional information, you can refer to the relevant sections of the SEND Code of Practice 2015:
SEND Code of Practice 2015: Annex 2 – Improving practice and staff training in education.

DCSF (2010) *Salt Review: Independent Review of Teacher Supply for Pupils with Severe, Profound and Multiple Learning Difficulties (SLD and PMLD).* Nottingham: DCSF Publications.

SSAT (2011) *The Complex Learning Difficulties and Disabilities Research Project: Developing Pathways to Personalised Learning, Final Report.* http://complexld.ssatrust.org.uk/uploads/CLDD%20research%20project%20(Final)%20Exec%20sum.pdf

Tutt, R. (2011) *Partnership Working to Support Special Educational Needs and Disabilities.* London: Sage.

White, E. and Jarvis, J. (2014) *School-based Teacher Training: A Handbook for Tutors and Mentors.* London: Sage.

Conclusions

This book set out to convey a sense of what the changes to the SEN Framework that occurred from September 2014 are all about, and to help readers to become familiar with the *2015 SEND Code of Practice: 0–25 years*, which interprets these changes for all those involved with children and young people who have special educational needs or disabilities. Part One of the book concentrated on painting a picture of what led up to the changes; the Children and Families Act that provided the legislative framework; and the contents of the SEND Code itself. In Parts Two and Three, a series of case studies were used to illustrate how schools, settings and services are working towards implementing the structural changes and the shift in culture that they represent

The cultural shift

Any cultural change does not happen overnight. While introducing new systems can have a timescale attached to them, it is less straightforward to dictate how long it may take to change hearts and minds. At the core of this cultural shift is the idea that children, young people and their families should be at the centre of the decisions that concern them and, furthermore, that they will be instrumental in helping to move forward the SEN system as a whole, so that it is in a state of continuous improvement rather than standing still.

Working in partnership with families

Over many years, there has been a gradual change in how professionals from across the services work with families. No longer are children and their parents or carers viewed as passive recipients, placing unwavering trust in a belief that the professionals know best. Today, the relationship is seen as more of an equal partnership, through which much more can be achieved. On the whole, schools and other educational settings have become used to this way of working, although the younger the child, the easier it is to welcome parents and carers into the school. Early years settings, primary and special schools, have the advantage that families want to keep in close touch. As young people move into secondary school and beyond, it is right that they become more independent and rely less on close parental support and involvement in their education. However, as the case studies have shown, it is no longer a case of making sure that parents have the opportunity to work in partnership with the school over their own child's progress, but all sorts of ways are being found of involving more parents and carers in the development of the school as a whole, including improving the capacity to meet the ever widening range of needs that are a feature of today's classrooms. Parents and carers are not just on governing bodies or helping to run the Parent Teachers Association (PTA), but taking a very active role in the strategic development of the school. In some cases, they may also be the means of encouraging parents and carers, who may not have happy memories of their own school days, to feel welcomed and valued.

Turning from parents to children and young people, schools and other settings have become more adept at listening to the voice of the pupils and giving them the opportunity to express their opinions. The case studies illustrated a number of ways this is being achieved, including setting aside a room where pupils can make a very short recording of what they want to say and staff are able to listen to these later and use the views they express to take any action that will improve the school from the point of view of the students. Even very young children have been shown to be encouraged to talk about their learning and how they can be helped to make progress. This is all part of taking seriously the idea that it is not just the views of the professionals that matter, but those who are on the receiving end of support can give valuable insights into how that support can best be delivered. If children feel encouraged from an early age to express their ideas, they will be readier to look beyond their own situation to how they can influence the work of the school or setting as a whole.

And beyond the influence that children and families can have at both the individual and school or setting level, is the drive to involve them in moving forward the SEN system as a whole. One way of achieving this is through their contribution to the development of the local authority's (LAs) Local Offer. In September 2014, LAs put their first attempts at producing a Local Offer on their websites and educational settings and other services have been contributing to its development. This means that, for the first time, there is one place where parents and carers can go to find the information they need about the support that is available to them and to their young people. Reference has been made in the case studies to how parents and pupils have been involved in this work and in the creation of the SEN Information Report that schools are required to produce. LAs have to publish parents' comments on their Local Offer and what they have done in response to those remarks. It is hoped that this feedback will lead to Local Offers being used as a mechanism to show what provision is lacking in a particular area and lead to improvements in the support available to children with SEND and their families.

In the same way that the first principle set out in the SEND Code of Practice is a reminder that the 'views, wishes and feelings' of children, young people and their parents must be borne in mind at all times, so this book has not sought to have a separate chapter devoted to them; instead their involvement is a theme throughout the book. Evidence from the SEND Pathfinders shows that a more collaborative approach to working with families makes them feel more in control, better informed and more satisfied with the services they receive. At the same time, professionals have found a genuine partnership with families can be very rewarding and generates better results. This may be particularly the case, as was shown in one of the case studies, for staff who have not been used to working face to face with families.

Working across education, health and social care

Working across the services is partnership working from a different angle. It is one that may be harder to achieve, as each service has different priorities. For instance, it could be that the health service is more concerned with meeting the needs of a growing population of the elderly and frail, than addressing the needs of the youngest generation. In addition, there are pressures on all three services, in terms of trying to stretch budgets and retaining enough staff.

On the positive side, since the Children Act of 2004, which was the last major attempt at inter-agency working, education and social care work have achieved a much closer working relationship. Local education authorities (LEAs) have been replaced by local authorities (LAs) covering both education and social care. So, this time round, there has been a real effort from the start of the changes, to tie health in to the new SEN framework. At government level, this has involved the DfE working closely with the Department of Health (DoH). This, in turn, has led to the creation of a number of posts for a Designated Medical Officer (DMO) or a Designated Clinical Officer (DCO). These people will be the link between the LA and Clinical Commissioning Groups (CCGs). LAs who have been working as SEND pathfinders have helped to lead the way in putting in place joint commissioning arrangements between the three services. The joint working that is needed to produce Education, Health and Care needs assessments and EHC Plans, means that a more joined-up way of working has begun to take root. Although the DMOs/ DCOs have only recently been appointed, some of the case studies show a greater involvement with health, for example, in supporting the education of children with complex medical conditions or mental health needs. Health professionals are also involved in some of the developments in provision for 19–25 year olds, who are now a recognised part of the SEN framework.

Working across children's and adults' services

The recognition that SEN support needs to continue up to 25 years is a very considerable step forward. Bringing FE colleges into the SEND Code of Practice will encourage the advent of a more co-ordinated system. Instead of two different arrangements for pre- and post-16, LDD (learning difficulties and disabilities) will no longer be used, but the term 'SEN' or 'SEND' covers the whole of the 0–25 age range. Learning Difficulty Assessments (LDAs) will disappear along with statements, as the universal term becomes EHC assessments and Plans. Having one system that spans children and adult services, should ensure a more seamless experience for young people and their families as they cross the post-16 threshold.

Although it is early days for implementing the changes, it is encouraging to see how current provision is being extended and new provision is being planned. Some of the schools and settings in the case studies have contributed to these developments. Clearly, provision for 19–25 year olds, which is where there is the greatest dearth of dedicated provision, cannot be an extension of a school, but has to be something different. Some interesting examples have been given that demonstrate what this provision can look like in terms of its relevance and effectiveness for this age group. One of the key elements is clearly to have a range of options to suit learners of very different abilities and interests. In time, this should lead to a considerable reduction in the number of young people with SEND who become NEETs (Not in Education, Employment or Training), many of whom have been only too keen to find work, but have been unable to do so.

Changes for educational settings

From the point of view of educational settings, other significant changes are: the change to a graduated approach called 'SEN Support'; the removal of BESD (behaviour, emotional and social development), and its replacement with social, emotional and mental health difficulties (SEMH); and making sure that every teacher is responsible for the progress of all the pupils in their class, including those who have SEN. Opinion has been divided about whether or not having SEN Support replacing School Action and School Action Plus is a better idea, but the case studies show that, where it is already being implemented, there are some positive benefits in being able to address needs sooner and bring in outside specialists as soon as they are needed (although there is a concern that cutbacks have meant the disappearance of some SEN Support Services and specialist teachers). There is general support for the idea that SEMH is a more helpful label, both in terms of concentrating on what is causing a child to behave in a certain way rather than simply focusing on their behaviour being problematic, and in terms of the recognition being given to mental health issues.

It is not always possible to have an environment that is ideal (although there were some fascinating examples in the case studies of how school premises have been developed inside and outdoors), but it is possible to improve what is there, to see it from the child's viewpoint and to make sure the setting they are in is a place where they feel safe, confident and are ready to learn. In this respect, every teacher seeing themselves as a teacher of SEND is one of the keys and leads on to the point made in the previous chapter that there has been a significant lack of training in this area from initial teacher training (ITT) onwards. The Carter Review of ITT that was mentioned in the last chapter, should lead to a greater consistency across the plethora of ITT routes that exists – and this is not to ignore the effectiveness of some schools, including teaching schools, whether special or mainstream, that have particular expertise in this area. The next stage needs to be a framework for CPD (continuous professional development), which sets out the different levels of training that are available. This would help to ensure that all teachers are expected to add to the knowledge and skills they acquired during their initial training; some teachers (in addition to SENCOs), would take training at a more advanced level, and some would go on to become specialists in an area of SEN, so that they could support colleagues across a number of settings. Some teachers have already followed this path, but what is needed is to raise the expectation that all teachers will be able to give meaning to the saying that every teacher is a teacher of children and young people who happen to have SEN or disabilities. There is more training available, including the online training mentioned in Annex 2 of the SEND Code of Practice, but it is left to individuals to seek it out and to compare different courses, rather than having an overarching framework.

Future prospects

It may not be the best time to change the Framework and to introduce a new SEND Code of Practice, as times are hard, and schools and other settings are faced with much else that is changing. On the other hand, there may never be a time that feels right, so, even though there will be constraints, at least the improvements can start to take shape. At the time of writing, implementation is just getting off the ground, but, already, it has been possible to show that opportunities are being grasped, new ways of working are beginning to emerge, and more humane attitudes are starting to take effect. This is the start of a journey that will lead, through closer working relationships between all those involved, not least between families and the professionals who are there to support them, to the emergence of a more effective and compassionate system.

References

Cheminais, R. (2011) *Family Partnership Working: A Guide for Education Practitioners.* London: Sage.

Cheminais, R. (2014) *Rita Cheminais' Handbook for SENCOs,* 2nd edn. London: Sage.

DCSF (2003) *Green Paper: Every Child Matters.* Nottingham: HMSO.

DCSF (2004) *Children Act.* Nottingham: HMSO.

DCSF (2005) *Mental Capacity Act.* Nottingham: HMSO.

DCSF (2007) *Planning and Developing Special Educational Provision: A Guide for Local Authorities and other Proposers.* Nottingham: DCSF.

DCSF (2008) *Special Educational Needs (Information) Act 2008.* London: HMSO.

DCSF (2009) *Lamb Inquiry: Special Educational Needs and Parental Confidence.* Nottingham: DCSF Publications.

DCSF (2010) *Salt Review: Independent Review of Teacher Supply for Pupils with Severe, Profound and Multiple Learning Difficulties (SLD and PMLD).* Nottingham: DCSF Publications.

DES (1970) *The Education (Handicapped Children) Act.* London: HMSO.

DES (1978) *The Warnock Report: Special Educational Needs: Report of the Committee of Enquiry into the Education of Handicapped Children and Young People.* London: HMSO.

DFE (1994) *Code of Practice on the Identification and Assessment of Special Educational Needs.* London: HMSO.

DfE (2010a) *Green Paper: Children and Young People with Special Educational Needs and Disabilities – Call for Views.* London: HMSO.

DfE (2010b) *The Equality Act.* London: HMSO.

DfE (2011a) *Support and Aspiration: A New Approach to Special Needs and Disability – a Consultation.* London: HMSO.

DfE (2011b) *Improving Alternative Provision: Charlie Taylor, Government's Expert Adviser on Behaviour.* London: HMSO.

DfE (2011c) *Munro Review of Child Protection: Final Report – a Child-centred System.* London: HMSO.

DfE (2012) *Support and Aspiration: A New Approach to Special Educational Needs and Disability – Progress and Next Steps.* London: HMSO

DfE (2014a) *Children and Families Act.* London: HMSO.

DfE (2014b) *A DfE Presentation Pack for School Leaders: The 0–25 Special Educational Needs and Disabilities Reforms,* www.sendgateway.org.uk/resources

DfE (2014c) *The Young Person's Guide to the Children and Families Act 2014,* www.gov.uk/government/publications

DfE (2014d) *Supporting Pupils at School with Medical Conditions*, www.gov.uk/government/publications

DfE (2014e) *Templates: Supporting Pupils with Medical Conditions*. Department for Education.

DfE (2014f) *Early Years: Guide to the 0–25 Code of Practice*, www.gov.uk/government/publications

DfE (2014g) *Further Education: Guide to 0–25 Code of Practice*, www.gov.uk/government/publications

DfE (2014h) *Schools: Guide to the 0–25 Code of Practice*, www.gov.uk/government/publications

DfE (2014i) *Statistical First Release: National Pupil Projections – Future Trends in Pupil Numbers: July 2014*, www.gov.uk/government/publications

DfE (2014j) *School Organisation (Maintained Schools)*, www.gov.uk/government/publications

DfE (2014k) *Statistical First Release: Special Educational Needs in England: January 2014*, www.gov.uk/government/publications

DfE (2014l) *Mental Health and Behaviour in Schools: Departmental Advice for School Staff*, www.gov.uk/government/publications

DfE (2014m) *School Exclusion Trial Evaluation: Research Report*, www.gov.uk/government/publications

DfE (2014n) *Carter Review of Initial Teacher Training (England): A Call for Evidence*, www.gov.uk/government/publications

DfE (2014o) *Social Care: Guide to the 0–25 SEND Code of Practice*, www.gov.uk/government/publications

DfE (2015) *Special Educational Needs and Disability Code of Practice: 0 to 25 Years*, www.gov.uk/government publications

DfE (2015a) *Carter Review of Initial Teacher Training (ITT)*, www.gov.uk/government/publications

DfE (2015b) *Government response to the Carter Review of Initial Teacher Training (ITT)*. www.gov.uk/government/publications

DfE/DoH (2014a) *Special Educational Needs and Disability Code of Practice: 0 to 25 Years*, www.gov.uk/government/publications

DfE/DoH (2014b) *Transition to the New 0 to 25 Special Educational Needs and Disability System: Statutory Guidance for Local Authorities and Organisations Providing Services to Children and Young People with SEN*, www.gov.uk/government/publications

DfE/DoH (2014c) *Implementing a New 0 to 25 Special Needs System: LAs and Partners*, www.gov.uk/government/publications

DfE/DoH (2014d) *0–25 SEND Code of Practice: A Guide for Health Professionals*, www.gov.uk/government/publications

DfE/DoH (2015) *Special Educational Needs and Disability Code of Practice: 0 to 25 Years*, www.gov.uk/government/publications

DfE/NCTL (2014) *Initial Teacher Training Criteria – Supporting Advice*, www.gov.uk/government/publications

DfES (2001a) *Special Educational Needs and Disability Act*. Nottingham: DfES Publications.

DfES (2001b) *Special Educational Needs: Code of Practice*. Nottingham: DfES Publications.

DfES (2003) *The Report of the Special Schools Working Group*. Nottingham: DfES Publications.

DfES (2004) *Removing Barriers to Achievement: The Government's Strategy for SEN*. Nottingham: DfES Publications.

Dittrich, W. and Tutt, R. (2008) *Educating Children with Complex Conditions: Understanding Overlapping and Co-existing Disorders*. London: Sage.

DoH (2005) *The Mental Capacity Act*. Nottingham: HMSO.

DoH (2014) *Care Act*, www.gov.uk/government/publications

House of Commons Education and Skills Committee (2005–6) *Special Educational Needs, Third Report of Session 2005–6*. London: HMSO.

House of Commons Health Committee (2002–03) *The Victoria Climbié Inquiry Report. Sixth Report of Session 2002–03*, www.pubications.parliament.uk

Jordan, R. (2013) *Autism with Severe Learning Difficulties, 2nd edn.* London: Souvenir Press.

Kaehne, A. (2014) *Final Report: Evaluation of Employment Outcomes of Project Search UK.* Liverpool: SWIE.

Kirby, A. (2013) *How to Succeed in College and University with Specific Learning Difficulties.* London: Souvenir Press.

Leslie, C. and Skidmore, C. (2007) *SEN: The Truth about Inclusion.* London: The Bow Group.

National College for Teaching and Leadership (NCTL) (2014) *National Award for SEN Co-ordination: Learning Outcomes.* National College for Teaching and Leadership.

Ofsted (2010) *The Special Educational Needs and Disability Review: A Statement is Not Enough.* Manchester: Ofsted Publications.

Ofsted (2011) *Alternative Provision Survey.* Manchester: Ofsted Publications.

Ofsted (2014a) *Initial Teacher Education Inspection Handbook.* Manchester: Ofsted Publications.

Ofsted (2014b) *School Inspection Handbook.* Manchester: Ofsted Publications.

Rose, J. (2006) *Independent Review of Primary Curriculum: Final Report.* Nottingham: DCSF Publications.

SSAT (2011) *The Complex Learning Difficulties and Disabilities Research Project. Final Report,* http://complexld.ssatrust.org.uk/uploads/CLDD%20research%20project%20(Final)%20Exec%20sum.pdf

Tutt, R. (2007) *Every Child Included.* London: Paul Chapman Publishing.

Tutt, R. (2011) *Partnership Working to Support Special Educational Needs and Disabilities.* London: Sage.

Tutt, R. and Williams, P. (2012) *How Successful Schools Work: The Impact of Innovative School Leadership.* London: Sage.

White, E. and Jarvis, J. (2014) *School-based Teacher Training: A Handbook for Tutors and Mentors.* London: Sage.

Index